NAPOLEONIC INFANTRY

NAPOLEONIC WEAPONS AND WARFARE

NAPOLEONIC INFANTRY

PHILIP J. HAYTHORNTHWAITE

CASSELL&CO

Cassell & Co
Wellington House, 125 Strand, London WC2R 0BB

First published 2001

British Library Cataloguing-in-Publication data:
A catalogue record for this book is available from
the British Library.

ISBN 0-304-35509-7

Distributed in the USA by Sterling Publishing Co. Inc.,
387 Park Avenue South, New York, NY 10016-8810.

Edited by Michael Boxall.
Design and layout by D.A.G. Publications Ltd., London.
Additional line illustrations by Terry Hadler.
Printed in Great Britain.

CONTENTS

The confusion of street-fighting: French infantry at
Aspern-Essling. (Print after F. de Myrbach.)

INTRODUCTION

WEAPONS AND TACTICS OF THE NAPOLEONIC WARS

As remarked, at somewhat greater length, in the introduction to the companion title, *Napoleonic Weapons and Warfare: Cavalry*, in order to comprehend the events of the Napoleonic Wars, and to appreciate the skills of the commanders, it is necessary to understand the most basic aspects of the warfare of that age: the capabilities of the weaponry, the manner in which troops fought, and how the two impacted upon each other.

Two primary sources might seem to give different perceptions of what actually happened upon the field of battle. The first of these consists of the technical specifications and theoretical performance of the weaponry, as recorded by contemporary tests, and of the manoeuvre-regulations which decreed how the sub-units of each army would operate, and the formations they would adopt. The second source, often less clear and sometimes difficult to interpret, are eyewitness accounts of what actually happened, and the many tactical discussions which occurred among military theorists at the time and in the years following the Napoleonic Wars. These discussions were often heated and sometimes proposed the impracticable, but in some cases they were the only reason why anecdotal accounts of what had actually occurred were ever recorded. The fact that many of these were written by British commentators may tend to give an uneven perspective, but many of their more general conclusions were of universal significance. It is not the intention here to detail in any depth the national patterns of weaponry or to recount the precise manoeuvre-regulations of each army, which are readily available elsewhere, but instead to examine some of the salient points of what occurred in practice, exemplified by contemporary experiences and opinions.

The extent to which the official manoeuvre- and drill-regulations were valid as a guide to what actually happened is debatable. There is no doubt that drill and training were essential to produce an efficient soldier, for only repeated drill and sometimes draconian discipline would enable an individual to stand in line and fire his musket almost like an automaton, and for units to retain the cohesion which was their only salvation, while all about them were scenes of indescribable carnage, great danger and an atmosphere of fear and confusion. One commentator remarked that discipline was 'nothing but each man, shoulder-to-shoulder, depending upon a whole, instead of himself alone', and which enabled 'even our sickly weavers and manufacturers [to be] useful to their country'[1] Most importantly, it also impacted upon the soldiers' confidence: confidence in his leaders, in his fellows who would stand with him, and in his own ability, the latter itself a product of his own training. Such confidence was essential for the maintenance of morale, the factor which was ultimately decisive on the day of battle.

Nevertheless, there must be a valid suspicion that what was decreed by the manoeuvre-manuals was not an infallible guide to what happened in practice. The basic ability to manoeuvre, form line, column and square was essential to maintain any sort of order; but beyond that, the more complicated manoeuvres of the type described by Ludlow Beamish as 'Chinese puzzles [which] only engross time and labour to the unprofitable end of forming useless combinations'[2] may rarely have been used: as one manual noted of a fairly complex manoeuvre, 'This looks well, and has a good effect on a day of parade; but it is too complicated to be attempted with safety in the presence of an enemy.'[3]

In some cases, even experienced troops may not have been proficient in the finer points of regulation manoeuvres, or officers may not have understood them. William Grattan recalled one commanding officer who, having got his men into square, was unable to get them out again, and who remarked, 'I can clearly discern that there is a something wanting', exhorted his officers to refer to Dundas's drill-manual, and told his confused troops, 'Men, you may go home.'[4] In other cases, there seem to have been quite deliberate variations in the official drill. Even for parade-ground manoeuvres a guide to Dundas's British drill-book noted that 'Some trifling Deviations from the "Rules and Regulations" ... are permitted in most Regiments',[5] and this was probably not exceptional. For example, prior to the War of 1812 various systems seem to have been used by American regiments, some commanders using a version of the French 1791 regulations and at least one, Dundas, in addition to the Steuben 'regulation' practice, and changes were introduced to take account of operating in wooded terrain. Indeed, some aspects of regulation manoeuvres seem to have been ignored entirely in practice, for example the almost universal use by the British infantry of a two-rank fighting-line at a time when three ranks were prescribed officially.

At times, regulation manoeuvres may even have been counter-productive: when his skirmishers were retiring in perfect order but too slowly at Talavera, Rowland Hill shouted, 'Damn their filing, let them come in anyhow.'[6]

Consideration must also be given to those forces which operated effectively without any prescribed manoeuvre-regulations, although these were almost always unable to stand against disciplined forces in the open field, but achieved success in situations particularly suited to them: the guerrillas in Spain and Tyrol are obvious examples.

Conversely, there were occasions when even the most complicated drill was put into practice on the battlefield, sometimes to the surprise of those who thought some parade-ground manoeuvres to be the 'useless combinations' referred to above. An example was quoted of how the French 63rd had to retire at Verona in 1799, falling back upon the 33rd and, using the prescribed drill, passing through it and re-forming behind it. Some had regarded the manoeuvre in question as applicable only to the parade-ground, but its value was proven in the heat of battle, and so, surely, were other complex manoeuvres throughout the period.

In studying the contemporary accounts of what actually happened, however, when troops were blinded by smoke and doubtless often so terrified that only the discipline of the parade-ground kept them in the ranks, there must be a suspicion that at times the confusion led to only a passing resemblance to what was prescribed in the drill manuals: Marshal Macdonald, for example, described French infantry under fire in 1813 and forming a 'square' which 'bore a striking resemblance in shape to an egg'![7] Such confusion and disorder recalls the remark made by General King to Prince Rupert, on seeing the latter's plan of his dispositions for the Battle of Marston Moor: 'By God, sir, it is very fyne in the paper, but ther is no such thinge in the ffields.'[8]

* * * * *

In this text it is practical to provide source-footnotes only to direct quotations. Wherever possible, English-language sources or English translations are quoted, to facilitate further study.

The wearisome nature of forced marches is exemplified in this depiction of Grenadiers à Pied of Napoleon's Imperial Guard, entitled 'Coquin de temps!' (Print after Horace Vernet.)

NAPOLEONIC INFANTRY

COMPOSITION

Although each army had its own systems and terminology, in general the infantry of all nationalities formed the most numerous part of an army and had a good deal in common in terms of organisation. The standard tactical unit was the battalion, though its strength might vary considerably both in establishment and, even more, in actual strength, especially after the attrition of campaign. For example, prior to the reforms supervised by the Archduke Charles, an Austrian battalion on war establishment was supposed to comprise some 1,380 'other ranks' (in practice often much fewer), whereas at the end of the 1811 campaign in the Peninsula the average strength of each of Wellington's battalions was only 550, ranging from 1,005 in the 1st Battalion 43rd to only 263 in the 2/38th. The precept that 'God is on the side of big battalions' (attributed to Turenne, and certainly repeated by Voltaire) was not always accurate, for a battalion might be so big that it became unwieldy. Marshal Auguste Marmont was among those who commented on this, remarking that French battalions were always too weak and Austrian ones too strong; and that the number of companies a battalion contained was not important, so long as when deployed in line every man should be able to hear the voice of the officer who commanded it, or else it was too big. Marmont's ideal proportion was one officer to every forty men; and for a thousand-strong battalion, he stated, only about 800 might be expected to take the field once the sick, depot and baggage-guards had been deducted, and this number would enable a unit to sustain considerable casualties but still remain effective.

The battalion might be only a component part of a regiment (though – as in the British army – many regiments comprised but a single battalion), but the regiment was generally only of administrative significance, the battalion remaining the primary tactical unit. The various battalions of a regiment might well take the field together: it often occurred in the French army, for example, where a brigade might be composed entirely of the battalions of a single regiment (in Davout's I Corps of the *Grande Armée* in 1812, for example, this was the case with fourteen of the sixteen brigades). This was generally of little importance; Marmont, for example, declared it irrelevant whether a regiment was composed of two or six battalions, except that as each regiment required a staff, it was more economical for one staff to superintend several battalions, and that with a greater number of battalions the depot for replacement of casualties might be more effective.

Battalions were composed of a number of companies, generally between six and ten, each with a maximum practicable strength of between 100 and 130 men. The company was originally an administrative unit, in the seventeenth century virtually the possession of its captain, who was responsible for its pay, recruitment and provisions, but by the late eighteenth century these had been taken over by the battalion or regimental administration, and the company was simply the principal tactical sub-unit of the battalion. It could be subdivided into half-companies, platoons (the German *Zügen*), or combined with another company to produce a 'division' (which should not be confused with the other meaning of this term, a grouping of a number of brigades). Within the battalion there might be 'élite' companies,

The effectiveness of the square was demonstrated at Prenzlau in 1806, when Prince August of Prussia's grenadier battalion repelled seven French cavalry charges by musketry from its second and third ranks at close range, the first rank kneeling with raised bayonets. (Print after Richard Knötel.)

ostensibly trained for a particular service; from their position when the battalion was drawn up in line, they were called 'flank companies' in English. Each battalion might possess one company of grenadiers, supposedly the most stalwart men with the best physique, and named from their use in the late seventeenth and early eighteenth centuries of hand-grenades; and a company of light infantry, supposedly the smallest, most nimble men, adept at skirmish tactics. The latter were generally a later creation than the grenadiers: French battalions, for example, only added a light company of *voltigeurs* (lit. 'vaulters') in 1804, although this was probably more the regularisation of a practice already widespread.

Alternatively, the 'élite' men might be deployed at regimental rather than battalion level, notably in 'Germanic' armies. Prior to 1806, for example, each Prussian regiment comprised one grenadier and two musketeer (line) battalions, but after that date they adopted the Austrian model, of having two separate grenadier companies in each regiment, to be detached and formed with the grenadier companies of other regiments into composite grenadier battalions. In Russian service each regiment comprised one grenadier and two musketeer battalions, with one of the four companies in each of the latter also being grenadiers; after the reorganisations of 1810–11 line regiments no longer included grenadier battalions, but the musketeer battalions retained their grenadier companies. The light infantry might also be deployed at regimental level rather than (as in British and French service) at battalion level; in Prussian service, for example, fusilier (light) battalions were originally separate entities, until the reorganisations of 1808 produced regiments composed of one fusilier (light) battalion and two musketeer battalions. There were also entire regiments of light infantry, though (as in French service) these were distinguished more by uniform and *esprit de corps* than by any marked difference in tactical abilities.

The formation of specialist units by detaching companies was not exclusively the preserve of those armies whose organisation was specifically directed towards it, for example the Austrian practice of always detaching the regimental grenadier companies. The system could also be applied on an *ad hoc* basis, either to form specialist units or simply to increase the number of tactical units within a small force, by the concentration of the élite companies into 'flank battalions'. Perhaps the best-known are the divisions commanded by Oudinot in Napoleon's army, known in 1805 as *Grenadiers de la réserve* and in 1806 and 1809 as *Grenadiers et Voltigeurs réunis*.

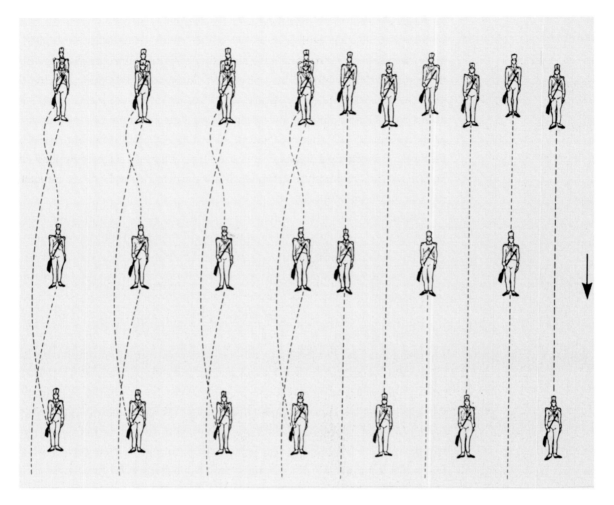

The terminology for the various types of infantry was varied. The ordinary companies were styled 'battalion' or 'centre' companies in British service (the latter from their position when drawn up in line). In French and Austrian service they were styled 'fusiliers' (from the French *fusil*, musket), though this term had other meanings. 'Fuzileers' (contemporary spelling) in British service was simply a title borne by three line regiments, relating to their origin as troops armed with light muskets (*fusils*) and implying nothing more than minor distinctions in uniform; in Prussian service fusiliers were the light infantry battalions; and in Russian service they were the 'centre' companies of grenadier regiments. Similar terms were used in other languages, for example *fucilieri* (Italian) and *fusileros* (Spanish), both indicating the ordinary 'centre' companies. The 'centre' companies of French light infantry were styled *chasseurs* (lit. 'hunters'),

Above: Light infantry drill: the British practice of advancing in extended order (right), and in extended order covering each other (left).

Below: French
grenadiers, although in
formation, firing at will,
probably typical of the
confusion which could
result when troops were
not ordered to fire by
volley. (Engraving after
Horace Vernet.)

the terms *cazadores* (Spanish) and *caçadores* (Portuguese) having the
same origin and meaning, although the similar German *Jäger* usually
implied rifle-armed troops. The 'grenadiers' of French light infantry were
styled *carabiniers*. The French term *tirailleurs* (sharpshooters) could be
used as an official title, but was equally applicable in a generic sense, to
describe any type of skirmisher. The German equivalent was *Schützen* and
the Portuguese *atiradores*, for example. The term 'musketeers' used to
describe Prussian and Russian 'centre' companies could have been used, as
in the seventeenth century, to classify any soldier armed with a musket,
though more generally had fallen from use.

Many actions must have been conducted in a somewhat irregular manner, as in this depiction of Marshal Ney leading the rearguard during the retreat from Moscow. (Engraving by H. Wolf after Adolphe Yvon.)

INFANTRY WEAPONS

MUSKETS

Consideration is given subsequently of the formations adopted by infantry, but with the exception of skirmishing, it should be remembered that the whole essence of infantry service was centred upon troops moving and fighting in compact blocks. Only by using such formations could units be kept together and manoeuvres executed, and they also determined the level of accuracy required from an ordinary musket: the central fact of weapons-technology was that nothing more precise was required of a musket than an ability to register a hit at some point upon a target very much larger than the proverbial barn door. This must have been a significant factor among a number of others which may have inhibited attempts to produce a more accurate firearm for the ordinary infantry.

The principal infantry weapon was the flintlock musket, sturdy and relatively simple to operate. Apart from some mentioned subsequently, the majority, of whatever nationality or pattern, were smoothbored muzzle-loaders. The musket comprised a tubular iron barrel affixed to a wooden stock (either by pins fitting through lugs soldered to the underside of the barrel, or by metal bands encircling both stock and barrel), with a small 'touch-hole' in the right side of the barrel through which a spark could penetrate from the outside to the propellant charge of gunpowder within. Placed by the touch-hole was the 'lockplate' on which the musket mechanism fitted. The spark was provided by a lump of flint, held in the jaws of a 'hammer' or 'cock' on the lockplate, striking against a hinged metal plate ('frizzen' or 'steel'), the cock being connected by an internal spring to the trigger on the underside of the stock. The striking of the flint forced back the hinged frizzen, thereby uncovering the 'priming-pan', a depression on the lockplate which contained gunpowder; ignited by sparks struck from the collision of flint and frizzen, this sent a flame to the interior of the barrel, igniting the propellant charge of gunpowder which sent the projectile on its somewhat uncertain flight. The projectile was a solid lead ball, roughly an ounce or less in weight; the size varied but was usually referred to as being of 'musket-bore' to differentiate it from the smaller 'carbine-bore', named after the cavalry firearm. Although loose gunpowder and balls could be used, that method was generally restricted to rifled weapons, ordinary muskets used a 'prepared cartridge', i.e. a paper tube containing a measured charge of gunpowder and one ball.

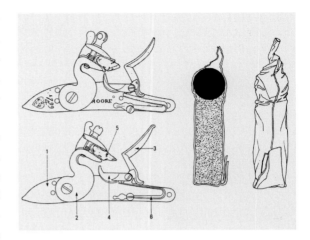

The firing drill was universal, even if the precise drill-movements varied slightly between armies. First, the soldier removed a cartridge from his cartridge-box or *cartouche*, a flapped leather pouch with a wooden or tin interior, usually slung over one shoulder. He then bit off the end of the cartridge, often retaining the ball in his mouth (hence the blackened faces – 'as black as if we had come out of a coal-pit'[9] – and raging thirst which afflicted soldiers in combat, from gunpowder getting in the mouth). Holding the musket horizontally, he drew back the hammer one notch to 'half-cock', at which point pressure on the trigger should have had no effect, unless it were faulty and 'went off at half-cock'. With the frizzen pushed back towards the muzzle, the priming pan was thus opened, into which a small amount of powder was poured and enclosed when the frizzen was moved into the vertical position. The musket-butt was then grounded, and with the

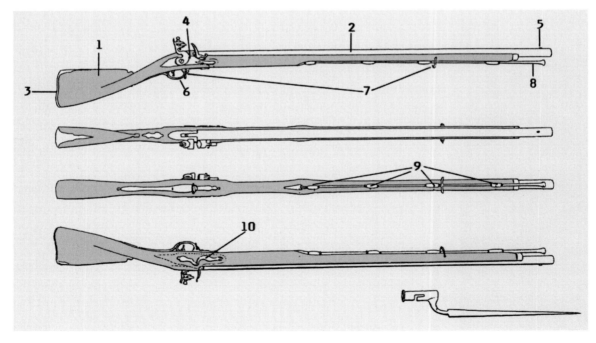

Left: *A typical flintlock, bearing the device of the British Honourable East India Company. Below this are the parts of a lock:*

1 *lockplate*
2 *cock or hammer (of 'swan-neck' type)*
3 *frizzen (or steel or hammer)*
4 *pan*
5 *flint*
6 *spring.*

On the right is a cartridge, showing cutaway of ball and powder. (In a 'buck and ball' round, three buckshot were usually positioned on top of the ball.)

Right: *The loading and firing drill, derived from one of the earliest illustrated drill-books,* William Windham's Plan of Discipline composed for the use of the County of Norfolk, *1759.*

Left: *The parts of a musket, an illustration derived from Windham's* Plan of Discipline for the Use of the Militia of the County of Norfolk, *1759.*

1 *butt*
2 *barrel*
3 *butt-plate*
4 *lock*
5 *sight*
6 *trigger-guard*
7 *sling-swivels*
8 *rammer*
9 *rammer-pipes*
10 *sideplate*

1 *Prime: the cock is drawn back one notch, and powder is poured into the pan, which is then closed.*
2 *Load: the rammer is withdrawn from beneath the barrel.*
3 *Load: the cartridge and ball is rammed down.*
4 *Load: the rammer is returned.*
5 *Make Ready: the musket is raised vertically.*
6 *Make Ready: the cock is drawn back on to 'full cock'.*
7 *Present Fire.*

barrel vertical, the powder from the cartridge was poured into it, followed by the ball. The soldier then removed the ramrod from its channel beneath the barrel, reversed it so that its bulbous end fitted into the muzzle, and rammed down the paper of the cartridge, holding the charge in place. The ramrod was then replaced and the musket returned to the horizontal, and the hammer drawn back an extra notch to 'full cock'. The musket was then raised to the right shoulder (it could not be fired from the left as the ignition of the powder in the pan would burn the face), levelled in the general direction of the enemy, and the trigger pulled; this caused the hammer to crash against the frizzen, opening the pan and showering sparks into it. The ignited powder passed into the barrel, and with a loud explosion and severe recoil the ball went on its way.

Although the firing-drill was standard, the national patterns of musket were considerably different, and indeed a considerable range of weapons might be carried within a single army. Perhaps the most famous was the British 'Brown Bess', a name perhaps deriving from the German *Büchse* (gun) and the practice of 'browning' the barrels, or simply a term of endearment. The alliterative nature of the nickname – even celebrated in a Kipling poem – perhaps contributed to its fame, though in reality the term referred to a range of firearms. The old 'Long Land Service' musket with 46in (116.8cm) barrel apparently lasted until 1790, despite the development in 1768 of the 'Short Land Service New Pattern' with 42in (106.7cm) barrel, which was the weapon generally in use at the beginning of the French Revolutionary Wars. Available supplies were inadequate for the rapid expansion of the army at that time, so the Board of Ordnance purchased some foreign weapons and, principally, a large quantity

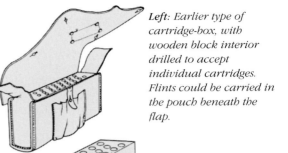

Left: Earlier type of cartridge-box, with wooden block interior drilled to accept individual cartridges. Flints could be carried in the pouch beneath the flap.

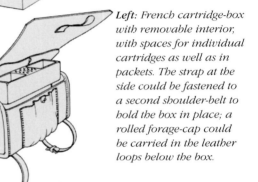

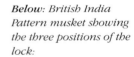

Left: French cartridge-box with removable interior, with spaces for individual cartridges as well as in packets. The strap at the side could be fastened to a second shoulder-belt to hold the box in place; a rolled forage-cap could be carried in the leather loops below the box.

Below: British India Pattern musket showing the three positions of the lock:
1 with pan open,
2 on half-cock with pan closed,
3 on full cock (the last two with flint removed).

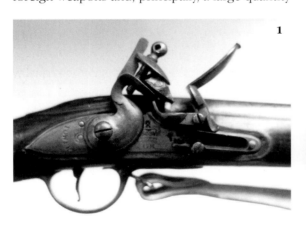

1

2

Right: *Firearms of distinctively Spanish design: top: musketoon with 'Catalan stock' of archaic design, and old-fashioned miquelet lock, as used by irregular troops and guerrillas; bottom: musket dated 1804, with a straight cock rather than the swan- or ring-neck style favoured by many other nations.*

Right: *British firearms, top to bottom: New Short Land Pattern (42-in barrel) (106.7 cm.); India Pattern (39-in: 99.1cm)barrel; New Land Service Pattern (42-in barrel); Baker rifle (30-in: 76.2cm) barrel, not drawn to common scale with the first three muskets. Bottom row: swan-neck and reinforced cocks; flat sideplate on Short Land Pattern; convex sideplate on India Pattern.*

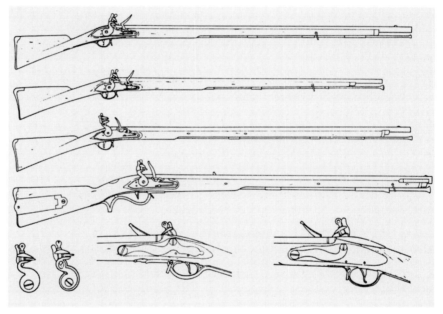

3

from the East India Company. The 'India Pattern' was somewhat inferior in manufacture, with a 39in (99.1cm) barrel and simplified fittings, but was easier to produce and of sufficient quality that in 1797 Ordnance gunsmiths were ordered to produce only India Pattern muskets. This remained the standard weapon (with the introduction of a reinforced cock in 1809), but other varieties continued to be produced, including a 'New Land Service' musket (plainer than the India Pattern and with 42in barrel), and from

1803 a Light Infantry musket with 39in barrel and a backsight (necessary for the more accurate aiming demanded of light troops). An attempt to produce a very superior musket, the so-called 'Duke of Richmond's' (named from the Master-General of Ordnance), designed by the great gunmaker Henry Nock and incorporating his 'screwless' or 'enclosed' lock (in which the working parts were all concealed behind the lockplate), was abandoned in 1798 because he was unable to produce them in sufficient quantity. (Some of the surplus locks were used up on cavalry carbines.) The number of British muskets produced was very considerable (more than 1.6 million India Pattern from 1804 to 1815, for example), and large quantities were sent abroad to arm the troops of Allied nations, not only to the Peninsula but to Prussia and Russia as well.

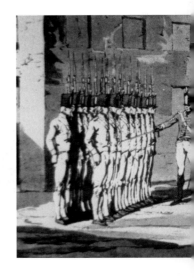

Probably equally well known was the French infantry musket, sometimes known as the Charleville (from one of the chief places of manufacture). It was essentially the Model 1777 with slight modifications, and was used throughout the period under the designations *An IX* and *An XIII*, Years 9 and 13 of the republican calendar (1800–1, 1804–5); about two million were produced. Varieties included a much-enhanced weapon with finer brass fittings and a stock with carved cheek-hollow, used by the Imperial Guard, and a short-barrelled version known as the *Vélite* musket. Large quantities of captured muskets were absorbed by French stores, and use was also made of the shorter Dragoon Musket by some *voltigeurs*, the reduced length being suited to skirmishing. The Charleville had a smaller bore than the 'Brown Bess' (equating to twenty balls to the pound against the British fourteen to the pound: 0.7in against 0.76in), which meant that British muskets could use captured French ammunition, but not vice versa. In June 1813, for example, Wellington complained that because of a delay

Below: French musket, An IX-XIII pattern: barrel-length 113.6cm (44.8 in), iron fittings.

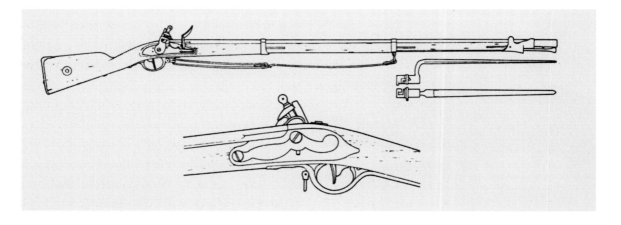

Above: Drill – the foundation of discipline. British infantry in their white undress jackets, with a 'fugleman' in front of the ranks, an exemplary soldier from whom the others took the timing of their drill. (Print after J. A. Atkinson.)

in receiving supplies, 'I am obliged to use the French ammunition, of a smaller calibre than our muskets, to make good our expenditure in the late action.'[10] The French musket was also lighter and had a more slender stock that the British equivalent. After the Battle of Vimeiro, G. B. Jackson, a subaltern in the British 43rd Light Infantry, was given the task of collecting and destroying French muskets, and recalled his surprise at how easily the stocks broke when smashed against a tree or rock. He thought that the French design sacrificed sturdiness and size of bore to reduce weight, though the latter was only of consequence in the context of a very long march, and while acknowledging that the 43rd and 52nd carried a superior type of 'Brown Bess', he thought the British musket in general markedly better than the French one.

Prussia used various patterns of musket, some of which featured conical touch-holes to facilitate loading. The 1782 pattern, use of which continued throughout the period, although with a modified butt, used the British system of construction, the barrel secured by pins. It was succeeded by the pattern of 1801 or 1805, known as the Nothardt, which had a reduced bore, though relatively small numbers were produced. The next pattern, known as the 'New Prussian' musket (*Neu-Preussisches Gewehr*) of 1809, was of superior quality, the barrel affixed by brass bands, and a brass pan with a shield to protect the user and his comrades from the flash, a feature also found on a number of muskets of other nations. A shorter musket (*Füsilier-Gewehr*) was used by light infantry (fusiliers), the 1787 version with a 95cm (37.4in) barrel, modified in 1796 by a 104cm (40.9in) barrel, but after Jena the fusiliers carried whatever was available, when Prussia had to use large quantities of captured weapons and those supplied by allied states, notably during the 'War of Liberation'.

In Austrian service, the 1784 musket was in use at the beginning of the French Revolutionary Wars: its calibre was 18.3mm and it was slightly lighter than the 1774 musket which was still in use. A notable distinction was for grenadiers' muskets to be stocked in polished walnut, the rest in stained beech, though probably the difference could not be maintained in wartime. A new musket was introduced in 1798, of improved construction, with brass

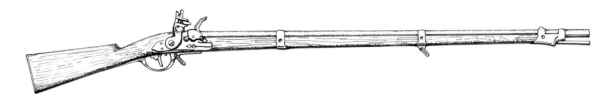

fittings and the calibre reduced to 17.6mm; the succeeding 1807 pattern was similar, but slightly lighter and with iron fittings.

According to contemporary observers, Russian muskets were among the worst in quality, with many calibres. The factories at Tula and Sestrovetsk produced between 150,000 and 170,000 per year, but quantity was no substitute for quality, and the Russian muskets were regarded as clumsy and inferior to those of other nations (so that the muskets supplied by the British were used to reward deserving soldiers). Although often styled a 'Tula' musket, the ironworks at that place was not dedicated exclusively to the manufacture of arms, but produced general works of considerable quality, even finely wrought furniture based on the designs of Thomas Sheraton, but executed in iron instead of wood.

The general performance of infantry muskets is perhaps best exemplified by the comments of George Hanger, a somewhat eccentric officer but a champion marksman:

> A soldier's musket, if not exceedingly ill bored and very crooked, as many are, will strike the figure of a man at 80 yards; it may even at a hundred; but a soldier *must be very unfortunate indeed* who shall be wounded by a *common musket* at 150 yards, PROVIDED HIS ANTAGONIST AIMS AT HIM; and, as to firing at a man at 200 yards

Above: Prussian musket, Model 1809 (the Neupreussisches-Gewehr); calibre, 19.3mm barrel-length 104cm (40.9in), brass fittings and pan, the lock fitted with a flash-guard.

Below: Russian infantry sabre; brass fittings, the grip with diagonal grooving and the blade with a narrow fuller.

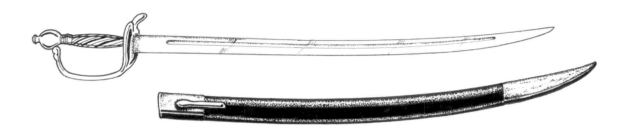

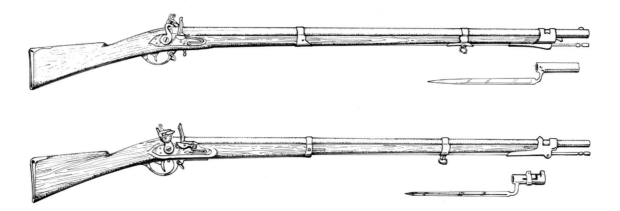

*Above: Austrian muskets.
Top, 1784 pattern; calibre
18.3mm, total length
150cm (59 in), iron
fittings.
Below, 1798 model;
calibre 17.6mm., total
length 150cm (59 in), iron
fittings but with brass
barrel-bands.*

with a common musket, you may as well fire at the moon and have the same hope of hitting your object. I do maintain, and will prove, whenever called upon, that NO MAN WAS EVER KILLED, AT TWO HUNDRED YARDS, by a common soldier's musket, BY THE PERSON WHO AIMED AT HIM.[11]

Confirmation of this statement may be found in many eyewitness accounts, perhaps most effectively by William Verner, who denied the common belief that a grey horse made its rider an especial target: because of the inaccuracy of musketry, he thought it was the grey-rider's companions who were most at risk, for while he might be aimed at especially by virtue of the prominence of his mount, the balls were sure to go wide and strike those around him![12]

The principal sources on the effectiveness of the musket are contemporary trials, and the accounts and opinions of those who observed the weapon in action. The results are considerably divergent as the test-data was obtained under ideal conditions and sometimes with muskets fixed in a rest, and might vary according to conditions, the size of the test and the experience of the shooters (French tests after the Napoleonic Wars, some conducted with percussion arms, suggest a wide range of results even under 'ideal' conditions.) Nevertheless, the test data is still significant. In the examples which follow, *approximate* metric measurements are given for those recorded in imperial measurements, and vice versa.

British tests in 1841 established the range of the 'Brown Bess' at between 100 and 700 yards (91 and 640 metres), though at every elevation there could be between 100 and 300 yards (91 and 274 metres) difference.

In another experiment a musket achieved a range of 1,030 yards (942 metres) at 45° elevation, but such statistics were irrelevant to what happened on the battlefield, where 300 yards (274 metres) might be regarded as the maximum practical range. The 1841 tests showed that at 150 yards (137 metres) a target twice as high and twice as broad as a man was hit three times out of four, but not at all at any greater range, nor were any hits registered on a target twice as wide at 250 yards (229 metres). Hanoverian tests of 1790, against a target equating to a line of infantry (50 yards long, 6 feet high) (46 x 1.82 metres) found that 75 per cent of shots hit at 100 paces, about 37 per cent at 200, and about 33 at 300; and against a similar target equating to a line of cavalry (8.5 feet high) (2.59 metres) the respective hits were about 83, 50 and 37 per cent. Prussian tests at the end of the eighteenth century, against a similar 'infantry' target 100 feet long (30 metres) registered about 60 per cent hits at 75 yards (68 metres), 40 per cent at 150 yards (137 metres) and 25 per cent at 225 yards (206 metres).

W. Müller, author of *Elements of the Science of War* (London, 1811), made a distinction between 'well trained' and 'ordinary' soldiers when conducting trials against a target representing a line of cavalry: at 100 yards (91 metres), 53 per cent by trained men, 40 per cent by ordinary; at 200 yards (183 metres) 30 and 18 per cent respectively; at 300 yards (274 metres) 23 and 15 per cent. French tests with a fixed musket, at a target 3 x 1.75 metres (10 x 5.7 feet) registered 60 per cent hits at 75 metres (82 yards), 40 per cent at 150 metres (164 yards), 25 per cent at 225 metres (246 yards) and 20 per cent at 300 metres (328 yards).

In addition to these 'national' trials, the Prussian general and reformer Gerhard von Scharnhorst published comparative details of the effectiveness of different national patterns, fired against a target 100 x 6 feet (91 x 1.82 metres) by ten men firing in their own time (i.e. not by volley). Some of the results were as follows, expressed as percentages of the total rounds fired:[13]

	100 paces	200 paces	300 paces	400 paces
Nothardt	72.5	48.5	28	33.5
New Prussian	74.5	52.5	29	16
French	75.5	49.5	26.5	27.5
British	47	58	37.5	27.5
Russian	52	37	25.5	29

Above: The Young Guard at Dresden: the man in the foreground is biting off the top of his cartridge to fill the open pan of his musket. (Print after Raffet.)

Statistics for effectiveness in combat are almost impossible even to approximate, but contemporary opinions certainly confirmed George Hanger's remarks, as quoted above. A traditional maxim held that for each enemy killed it required the expenditure of seven times his own weight of shot. A Prussian commentator stated that to put a soldier *hors de combat* required his own weight in lead and ten times his weight in iron (bullets and artillery rounds respectively), and claimed that taking the two together and excluding the Swedish artillery, which he thought the best in Europe, for precision of fire the British were the best and the French the worst. Another held that one musket-shot in 400 took fatal effect in battle, and another claimed that only one shot in 236 took effect at Tournai in 1794, and one in 300 at Oulard in 1798. (These statistics demonstrate the difficulties of accepting contemporary opinions without question. The Tournai calculation must have been taken from Mason's *Pro Aris et Focis*, a treatise on the use of bow and pike, and was based upon the premise of 40,000 Allied infantry each firing thirty-two rounds, causing half the 10,000 total enemy casualties. The actual statistics would suggest a maximum of about 20,000 infantry causing a proportion of about 5,500 casualties, which if half *were* caused by infantry fire the original calculation would not be too far out, though certainly not sufficiently accurate to give so precise a figure – even leaving aside the fact that the original calculation should have been 256! Oulard is also not an ideal case, in that it was an action contested between partly trained militia and civilian insurgents.) The head of the British Field Train in the Peninsula, R. Henegan, calculated that at Vittoria the Allied infantry used some 3,675,000 rounds to cause some 8,000 casualties, one hit per 459 shots, which does not include the effect of the 6,800 artillery rounds fired; and at every Peninsular battle, save Barrosa, he noted 'the same undue expenditure of ammunition in relation to the small extent of damage done'.[14]

Two factors which made the effectiveness of musketry so poor were the construction of the weapon and the nature of its projectile. George Hanger claimed that only one shot in 200 might be expected to take effect because 'the soldiers' muskets are all crooked, and if, per chance, a few be tolerably straight bored, they are bent in soldering the loops on'.[15] A more definite cause of inaccuracy was 'windage', the difference in diameter between bore and projectile, a looser-fitting ball moving laterally in the barrel as it was propelled forwards and so deviating more from the direction in which it was aimed. The effect of windage was demonstrated by the distinguished scientist Benjamin Robins (1707–51) in the 1740s, his comparison between tight-fitting musket-balls and the looser-fitting type favoured by the military (for ease of loading) being quite striking. Robins used a musket fixed in a rest, propelling a ball through two tissue-paper screens, 50 and 100 feet (15 and 30 metres) from the musket, and on to a wall 300 feet away (91 metres). He discov-

Above: In the firing-line: Prince Wilhelm of Prussia (later Kaiser Wilhelm I) with Prussian infantry at Bar-sur-Aube. (Print after C. Röchling.)

ered that the trajectory of successive balls, propelled by equal charges of powder, varied enormously to right and left of the aiming-mark, a tight-fitting ball having a 'spread' of 86 inches (2.18 metres) and a loose-fitting ball a 'spread' of 117 inches (2.97 metres) at 300 feet – one ball striking 94 inches (2.38 metres) right of the aiming-mark, another 23 inches (58 cm) left. These tests involved only five shots with each type of ball. Taking an average deviation from the aiming-mark (a statistic not conclusive due to the small number of shots fired) Robins's statistics may be expressed thus:[16]

Deviation at	50 feet	100 feet	300 feet
Tight ball	3.8 in (9.6cm)	7in (17.7cm)	30in (76.2cm)
Loose ball	9.8 in (24.8cm)	17in (43 cm)	49in (124.4cm)

Subsequent tests confirmed the considerable effect of windage. Trials in France in 1814 compared muskets using balls of 18 and 20 to the pound (the latter with greater windage) and a modified Versailles (rifled) *carabine*; the latter proved to be four times more accurate than the musket using balls of 18 to the pound, but twelve times more accurate than those using 20 to the pound. Another test, against at target at 83 yards' range (76 metres), showed that over that distance a loose-fitting ball had more than twice the aberration of a close-fitting ball. Excessive windage also caused loss of velocity, demonstrated perhaps most strikingly by the case of a 24pdr cannon-ball, when a windage of only 0.14in caused a loss of power of one-third of the propellant charge. Despite claims that increased windage provided greater ease of loading, tests in the 1840s with an American musket and balls of minimum windage fired 100 rounds without any difficulty from fouling.

Opinions were divided on the merits of heavier or lighter balls, the performance of which depended not only upon their own weight but upon the quantity of propellant powder. Tests were conducted to determine the effect of gravity, heavier balls having a tendency to drop to a greater extent, and thus have a reduced maximum range when compared with a lighter ball using the same charge. The difference could be striking: a test with later percussion muskets fixed at an elevation of 15° found that a musket using balls of 18 or 19 to the pound threw its projectile about 1,400 yards (1,280 metres), but with 14½ balls to the pound, only 860 yards (786 metres). It was noted that an increase in the propellant charge to compensate for the heavier ball was not feasible because of the additional recoil, and 'even now the recoil is severe, so much so, that a portion of the powder is often clandestinely thrown out of the cartridges'.[17]

Another test – again conducted with muskets later than those of the Napoleonic Wars – was against a target 6 x 2 feet (1.82 x 0.6 metres) at 300 yards (274 metres) range. With the heavier ball, 76 per cent of shots fell short and 8 per cent hit an area around the target measuring 30 x 6 feet (9.1 x 1.82 metres). With the lighter ball, 42 per cent fell short, 46 per cent hit the area around the target, and 2 per cent actually hit the target itself. (The individual chosen to fire was familiar with fowling-pieces but not with military muskets, and the muzzles were supported, presumably so that his fatigue would not be a factor. The recoil of the musket with the heavier ball was such that it gave him a bloody nose!)

In 1821 a Prussian comparison of British and French muskets claimed that the French (20 balls to the pound, less windage, charge one-half the weight of the ball, greater velocity) resulted in reduced range and less precision of fire than the British (14 balls to the pound, charge one-third the weight of the ball). Other factors were more difficult to determine. It was claimed that the reduced charge used by the British caused less fouling and therefore reduced the misfire rate, and that the reduced recoil gave the soldier less cause for hesitation and therefore greater accuracy.

Although it was possible for ammunition with minimum windage to be produced, some thought it undesirable, because the musket was for use 'against numbers, in close order, when aiming at individual men is neither practicable nor requisite, and the main point therefore, rapid and steady firing ... which require[s] a quick and easy method of loading, and consequently with cartridge and its loose-fitting ball, which of itself is rather incompatible with good marksmanship, but being essential for the real business of war, any decrease of windage that should at all affect this facility in loading, would turn out to be most seriously disadvantageous'.[18]

As recoil was dependent upon the weight of the weapon, powder and lead, some held that whatever diminished the charge was desirable, so that a lighter ball would increase accuracy as well as range; one commentator claimed than American smoothbores using balls of 30 to the pound were three times more accurate than those using 14 to the pound. Adherents of the larger ball claimed that it was more lethal, doing more damage than a light ball; to which one author retorted, that this would have the effect only of retarding the convalescence of an injured man, whereas the main object of shooting at the enemy was to put him *hors de combat* on the *day of battle*, so that a lighter ball would be equally effective and would have a longer range.

Below: Musket-drill: a member of Napoleon's Young Guard (left), who reaches behind him to extract a cartridge from his cartouche, while an Old Guard grenadier (right) aims. (Print after Charlet.)

(Differing calibres of muskets, however, could create great problems in the field: in 1805, for example, when Austria supplied munitions to Kutuzov's army, the smaller Austrian calibre meant that the musket-ammunition was apparently supplied in its raw state – loose powder and lead ingots – so that the Russians had no choice but to manufacture their own cartridges.)

Recoil was certainly ferocious, as testified by several soldiers: 'I now felt rather sore from firing my piece so often; the recoil against my shoulder and breast had blackened them, and rendered them rather painful, and the middle finger of my right hand was completely blackened and swoln [sic] from the same cause.'[19]; 'I could scarce touch my head with my right hand; my shoulder was as black as coal'[20] (after firing 108 rounds). Attempts to reduce recoil by surreptitiously pouring some of the gunpowder on to the ground before loading would only have served to reduce range and striking-power even further.

At the end of its course, a musket-ball might strike a person but not even penetrate his clothing; at this time it was termed a 'spent ball' and there are numerous accounts of men being hit but hardly suffering even a bruise. (Nevertheless, a spent ball could cause temporary incapacitation: a member of the British 71st recalled how at Toulouse he collapsed, sick and faint, after being hit by one in the groin; he was overtaken by the pursuing French and would have been killed had not one of the enemy recognised him as having saved his life earlier in the war, so instead of bayoneting him, gave him a pancake.)

The noise of flying bullets was remarked by a number of writers, young soldiers sometimes mistaking it for the buzzing of bees or the drone of beetles. Cavalié Mercer recalled how his battery's surgeon at Waterloo, under fire for the first time, amused the veterans by remarking, 'My God, Mercer, what is that? What is all this noise? How curious! How very curious!'[21]

Spent balls sounded different; one who described the sensations of being under fire wrote of 'the long melancholy whistle of the spent balls; but, as we approached nearer the enemy, they flew past in full force, with a noise resembling the chirping of birds'.[22] An even more bizarre description was given by Goethe, who said that in addition to the humming and whistling of balls, the air seemed so hot that although his vision remained unimpaired, the world seemed to assume a brownish-red hue, all the more remarkable in that the only direct physical sensation was that experienced by the ears, in the noise of flying shot.

Balls were not the only projectiles which could be fired from a muzzle-loader, but virtually anything which fitted into the barrel. Some truly bizarre incidents are recorded: at Vimeiro, Rifleman Brotherwood of the British 95th, having run out of balls, fired his razor at the French, and contemporary press-reports describe fatal injuries being sustained by projectiles as curious as a pewter spoon and a wooden ruler. At close range even the wadding of a cartridge could be lethal: Captain L'Olivier of the Belgian 7th Line was wounded by a cartridge-paper wad at Waterloo, an actor was killed at Preston in 1802 by the wadding of a blank fired on stage, and in 1795 a man in Edinburgh was killed by a plug of chewed tobacco shot at him for a joke.

Some particularly fearsome projectiles are recorded. At Saragossa Baron de Marbot was shot by a serrated-edged slug fired from a blunderbuss, calculated to do much more damage than a conventional ball. Having entered near the heart and been extracted close to the spine, this curious object was sent to Napoleon for inspection, after which he sent it as a souvenir to Marbot's mother. Accounts exist of balls being cut to make the metal expand; Wellington commented that 'I think that the Spanish Guerillas practised this method. I can recollect that the Impression upon our minds at the time was, that it was not fair. That Impression may have been erroneous. It is certain that the Wound received was a bad one.'[23] Something similar may have occurred in 1809 when an officer of the French 26th *Léger* survived being shot at Ebersberg by a missile which expanded to make a 3-inch hole. A load comprising a mixture of ball and buckshot was commonly used in America in the War of 1812, and something similar was produced in Egypt in 1807. Under desperate circumstances at El Hamet, a beleaguered British force opened many cartridges to use the powder for artillery, the spare balls being chopped up so that in addition to his ordinary musket-ball, each man fired three or four slugs to make his shot as devastating as possible. Their Ottoman opponents used a load just as unorthodox, two balls connected by a piece of wire, which caused fearful gashes if they hit.

George Hanger advised that when firing at troops who had broken, a rifleman should load two balls at once, and 'never fire at a single man, but fire with steady aim, where you see them huddled together, and crowded in lumps',[24] presumably in the hope of hitting more than one man! William Surtees, with the British 56th Foot in the Netherlands in 1799, recalled being so angry with the enemy for their successes that he deliberately loaded with two balls at once, to do them the maximum damage.

Among other factors which influenced the performance of muskets was the design of the weapon itself. Although some thought the ordinary musket too heavy, it was stated that the weight helped absorb recoil, which

Above: 'The fog of war': the immense cloud of smoke generated by musketry, depicted in this scene of volley-firing at a field day in Hyde Park. (Print after Thomas Rowlandson.)

would be so great with a lighter musket that a reduced charge would be needed, in turn reducing the effective range. Nevertheless, one advocate of a lighter musket, firing a smaller ball from a shorter barrel, claimed that not only would the soldier be able to carry more rounds, but that the reduced charge would eliminate some of the 'fog of war' caused by powder-smoke, and that a barrel of about 30 inches (76cm) would enable the musket to be loaded from a kneeling position. (This was difficult with a longer musket; indeed, a short man might have trouble with a very long barrel even when standing. Some illustrations of loading-drill depict the musket held almost vertically, whereas it was probable that at times it was held at a considerable angle, to facilitate reaching the muzzle.) Lighter muskets were certainly favoured for light troops or for 'irregular' warfare. One Peninsular campaigner remarked that light fusils, weighing about 6 pounds, such as used by Spanish smugglers, were far more suitable than the ordinary musket for such service (the 'Brown Bess' and bayonet weighed about 14 pounds.): 'Any one who has ever pulled a trigger will at once perceive how ill adapted a bar of iron, yclept a British musket, is for such a system of warfare. Yet these muskets were sent out to Spain by the Ordnance Department during the war, by hundreds of thousands, at vast expense to England, to be thrown away by the Spaniards the first convenient opportunity.'[25]

Even the shape of the stock had an effect: Scharnhorst's trials, for example, showed a marked improvement in the accuracy of the Prussian 1782 musket when fitted with a butt which facilitated aiming. Quality of manufacture was also remarked: for example, one British officer recalled at Waterloo seeing soldiers trying to find a better lock among muskets dropped by casualties, and even hurling away bad muskets in a rage. Among complaints was that the lock could be too strong, making even pulling the trigger difficult, which, 'in nine cases out of ten ... makes the soldier open the whole of the right hand in order to aid the action of the forefinger; this gives full scope to the recoil: the prospect of the blow makes him throw back his head and body at the very moment of giving fire; and, as no aim is ever required, he shuts his eyes, from the flash of the pan, at the same instant, so that the very direction of the shot becomes a matter of mere accident'.[26] It was said that the strength of the spring caused the flint to strike harder than necessary, so that the frizzen became scored and cut. This was exacerbated by the practice of fixing the flint into the hammer with a piece of lead, screwed in as tightly as possible; leather was preferable to lead, it was said, and the screw should only have been tightened sufficiently to hold the flint in place, to provide a little 'give' and thus damage the frizzen less. The same factor affected the efficiency of the flint, which it was said was only really good for ten or twelve shots before it began to deteriorate. A damaged flint could be reshaped by chipping at it with the turnscrew used to service the lock, and Surtees wrote with feeling about the bad quality of the ordinary musket and the paucity of supply of flints, 'which may be almost had for an old song; but ... many a brave soldier has fallen while hammering at a worn out flint'.[27]

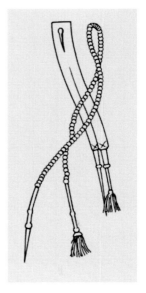

Above: Wire brushes and 'pickers', used to clean the touch-hole and pan of a musket.

Misfires (when the powder failed to ignite) were common, generally caused by insufficient sparks from the flint, damp powder or a blocked touch-hole; a musket which thus 'hung fire' could be very dangerous until the charge had been extracted or it had been persuaded to ignite. A British test under ideal conditions suggested a misfire rate of one in $6^1/2$ shots, while in 1796 it was claimed that 20 per cent misfires could be expected from the badness of the flints and the softness of the metal from which frizzens were made; and it was added that this had an adverse effect upon morale if soldiers thought their muskets so useless. Cartridges might also be defective, the paper being easily damaged, so that there are references to soldiers taking care to replace imperfect ones before an action. Commenting on the rapidity with which cartridges were used in combat, an Austrian writer remarked that many were dropped accidentally and either trodden or soaked if the ground were wet, so that a infantryman's common allocation of sixty might be exhausted without them all being fired. In this, especial criticism was made of the position of the cartridge-box, commonly carried at the rear of the right hip, where its uneven distribution of weight caused fatigue, and being unable to see what he was doing, it was easy for the soldier to dislodge more cartridges than he wanted as he reached behind him, losing some on to the ground. Recommended alternatives were belts containing rows of tubes which went around the body, as used in Calabria and Corsica, or to transfer the cartridge-box to the front; but in fact only very limited use was actually made of such so-called 'belly-boxes'.

Musketry could also be adversely affected by unsuitable weather. Tests carried out with rifle-balls fired in a strong cross-wind (published 1831) found that using a bullet of 19 to the pound, at 315 yards (288 metres) the wind (strength not specified) caused a divergence of between three and four feet. In very wet weather a musket might become entirely inoperable through rain-soaked powder, which accounts for instances of squares being broken by cavalry, the infantry unable to defend themselves against lancers, who could outreach their bayonets.

An experience which exemplified the problem was recorded in China in 1841, when a party of the 37th Madras Infantry was rendered helpless by torrential rain and compelled to retreat before an enemy whose spears outreached their bayonets. When the rain stopped, however, 'Many of the Sepoys, after extracting the wet cartridge, very deliberately tore their pocket handkerchiefs, or lining from their turbans (the only dry thing about them), and baling water with their hands into the barrels of their pieces, washed and dried them. They were then enabled to fire a few volleys.'[28] One of the Chinese, armed with a matchlock musket, picked up one of the loaded but inoperable flintlocks, opened the pan, turned over the wet powder to find a dry morsel and applied to it his own smouldering slow-match, which caused the powder to ignite and sent the ball into the arm of a British officer. In these exceptional circumstances the more archaic form of firearm proved more effective than the 'modern' flintlock!

A different problem was encountered when a musket had been fired repeatedly: it could become so hot as to be unsafe to load lest the powder ignite prematurely. Tests carried out by William Duane in America found that after twenty-five shots without a pause the barrel became so hot that the musket could only be handled by the sling or stock, and Jean-Roch Coignet recalled how at Marengo, 'There was nothing for it but to piss into the barrels to cool them, and then to dry them by pouring in loose powder and setting it alight unrammed.'[29] If a touch-hole became clogged with burned powder – the coarser French powder was said to cause more fouling than the British – it had to be cleared with the 'pricker' or needle carried by each soldier, sometimes suspended from the centre of the shoulder-belts to be within easy reach.

Another factor which radically reduced the effectiveness of musketry was the inadequate training given to infantrymen. Charles James Napier averred that the musket could be used in the field effectively by a boy of fifteen, and in a fortification by a boy of ten; but this ability was often undermined by lack of practice, especially with live ammunition. In British service, for example, line regiments received thirty rounds of ball and seventy of blank, per man per year, but only light infantry received tuition in target-practice. Other armies were even more parsimonious: in 1805, for example, Austria attempted to train recruits with only six rounds per man. Sir John Moore, who played an influential role in the development of light infantry tactics in the British Army, noted that the essentials were to load quickly without interfering with the adjoining men: 'That of firing is in the Level [aiming] – The men should be taught always to look along the piece, and to take aim, before they draw their trickers [sic]', and that practice without powder and with blanks was useful, but only firing with ball at a target could teach shooting properly. [30] Wooden flints could also be used for practice, these being termed 'snappers' in British service. ('Snapping' was evidently a colloquial term for 'snapping' the lock without actually firing; the East Yorkshire Regiment earned the nickname 'the Snappers' from an incident in the War of American Independence, when as the 15th Foot, having exhausted their ammunition, they merely 'snapped' at the enemy, perhaps using small charges of their remaining powder, to convey the impression of a continuing fusillade.)

It was acknowledged that certain men had an inherent skill in weapons-handling, for example 'the backwoodsmen of America, or the foresters of Germany, trained to the practice from infancy' according to the British tactical writer John Mitchell, and for those who had not been taught to shoot earlier, 'good instruction must make up for that disadvantage; but the present mode of drill only tends to make men bad shots'.[31] The most serious failing was probably an inability to aim. Although aiming at an individual was futile, some care was needed to 'level' the musket correctly, though few had any rear-sight and the front-sight was hidden when the bayonet was fixed (the weight of the bayonet made aiming even more difficult). Hardly any instruction seems to have been given in judging distances, and so gauging the fall of shot due to gravity (it was calculated that an ordinary ball would drop five feet in 120 yards; 152cm in 110 metres). William Surtees remarked that eight out of ten soldiers would aim in the same way at a target 50 yards away (46 metres) as at one at 300 yards (274 metres), which was why he reckoned that only one shot in 200 ever took effect. Some commentators remarked on how troops should aim at a different part of their target's anatomy according to distance and to compensate for the fall of shot, but little practical training seems to have been given, and indeed volley-firing was not conducive to aiming, as by firing on command men might pull the trigger before they were properly ready. One commentator criticised the practice of raising the barrel and bringing it down to the level required, claiming greater accuracy for raising it up and firing as soon as it came in line with the target, for as soon as the movement ceased the weight of the gun would tend to make the barrel shake.

A very common failing seems to have been the tendency to fire high. John Patterson, a Peninsula veteran, declared that 'nothing could be more absurd than the mode in which our soldiers usually give their fire in action; for, whether it be owing to the improper mode of training at ball-practice, or from any other cause, they fire considerably above the mark. Scarcely one shot in a thousand ever tells. Quantities of ammunition are thus uselessly expended.'[32] He suggested this in relation to the 43rd Light Infantry at Vimeiro, to which G. B. Jackson, doubtless anxious to preserve his regiment's reputation, replied that the only men who fired high were those shooting at French sharpshooters hidden in the tops of trees! Jackson recalled that during this action, the officers were constantly calling 'Fire low!', 'Aim steady!', 'Fire low!', which was how the 43rd had been trained,[33] and there are many accounts of similar exhortations. Daniel Nicol, for example, recalled how in Egypt 'General Doyle desired us to lie close to the ground until ordered to rise, telling us in an Irish whisper to level low, for said he, one bullet in a Frenchman's shin bone this day is as good as two in his head some other time.'[34] Similarly, when ordering his 28th Foot to fire by platoons (from centre to flanks) at Barrosa, Sir Charles Belson exclaimed, 'Be sure to fire at their legs and spoil their dancing.'[35]

Nevertheless, a number of accounts mention musketry going far too high. Thomas Austin described an action at Merxem in 1814 during which the combatants were barely twenty paces apart (though it was at night), when the enemy fired so high that almost the only hits were balls passing through the men's shakos, and even when this became a musketry duel, when the French would have the opposing musket-flashes at which to aim,

Left: Auxiliary troops formed a considerable proportion of many armies of the Napoleonic era: a member of the Lisbon Police Guard (left) and an Algarve militiaman of the Portuguese army, c. 1809. (Engraving by I. Clark after H. Michel.)

their fire was so high that it caused only a few scalp wounds. Another incident occurred at Cazal Nova (March 1811) when British skirmishers breasted a rise and came 'within a few yards' of a French regiment, which 'fired a volley in our faces. It was quite ridiculous; the balls went whizzing over our heads, and they scampered off.'[36] It is likely that both the stress of combat and the nature of the terrain contributed to such ineffectual musketry. The terrain was probably a factor in the attack of the British 39th at Garris in the Pyrenees in 1814, when as they advanced in close column along a ravine they came under heavy fire from above, but although the noise of the balls striking the trees alongside the column made a most peculiar sound, the firing was so high that only the mounted officers were hit. Similarly, Charles James Napier remarked on a particularly effective fire delivered on one occasion by the British 88th, 'because the ground formed an inclined plane, at the lowest part of which stood the British regiment, and therefore every shot told, not a ball passed over the heads of the enemy who stood above them on the ridge';[37] the range was about 60 yards (55 metres). Conversely, firing with an elevated trajectory might increase musket-range: at Arcangues in December 1813, for example, the British 43rd drove back two French batteries at a much greater range than normal (about 400 yards; 365 metres) by volley-firing from the upper storey of a church.

Further reductions in the efficiency of musketry were caused by soldiers' incompetence, or panic in the heat of battle. In his *Mémoires*, Marmont recounted the extreme case of two young conscripts in action at Champaubert, one of whom was not using his musket though balls were flying all around him. When questioned, he replied that 'I can shoot as well as the next man, if I have someone to load my musket'; 'The poor child was so ignorant of his business,' remarked Marmont. The second conscript handed his musket to his lieutenant, who *did* know how to fire, and he shot while the lad stood beside him, betraying no fear, and handed him the cartridges. The stress of combat could cause mistakes in the firing-drill. One hazard was over-priming (putting too much powder in the pan): even at a field day in Hyde Park in 1796, a guardsman 'had his eye nearly blown out' by a neighbour's musket,[38] for example, and at Waterloo William Lawrence recalled how his adjoining man had over-primed his lock. When he fired, a shower of burning powder hit Lawrence in the face, where he already had a slight injury from a shell-splinter, which 'soon made me dance for a time without a fiddle'![39] After a misfire a confused soldier might continue to load; a case was recorded in 1804 when a member of the Tower Hamlets Militia at

Above: The manoeuvre of troops in compact bodies on the battlefield, half-concealed by smoke, is shown to good effect in this depiction of the battle of Nivelle. (Print by Sutherland after William Heath.)

Blackheath rammed in cartridge after cartridge, which finally ignited on the fifth attempt, killing him and severely injuring seven others. In haste, a ramrod might be fired away accidentally, preventing the musket from being used as well as presenting a danger to those in the vicinity: 'while the ramrod was in the barrel, the piece was accidentally discharged. The ramrod pierced through his body, and so firmly was the worm-end near the backbone, that the strongest man among us was unable to move it.'[40] (John Kincaid added that it was eventually hammered out with a stone, and amazingly the man recovered!)

Another problem stemmed from short-cutting the loading drill, which must have exacerbated the misfire rate: by simply inserting powder and ball into the muzzle and then banging the butt upon the ground, trusting that it would shake enough powder into the priming-pan, thus greatly speeding the time taken to load. One British officer commended this practice, remarking that by using it French skirmishers could fire twice as rapidly, and that it was astonishing how effective such ultra-rapid fire was if one had to endure it, but others decried the practice. Commanders had been bemoaning such laziness since at least the time of the Earl of Orrery's *The Art of War* (1677), and in 1726 General Henry Hawley remarked that although German and Dutch troops might be prevailed upon to load properly, 'by the nature of our men, I believe it impossible to bring them to it'.[41] Remarking on the ineffectiveness of British musketry at Waterloo, Edward Cotton thought that it 'might be attributed to many of our infantry, when hard pressed, adopting the French skirmishers' method of loading, viz., giving the butt a rap or two on the ground, which, from the rain, was quite soft. The ball, in consequence, not being rammed down to confine the powder, came out nearly harmless.'[42] G. B. Jackson suggested another hazard of the practice, after examining French muskets at Vimeiro, of which a considerable number had burst, which he attributed to this form of loading, which 'might do while the barrel was clear, but after a few discharges, the cartridge would be apt to stick on the way, and the frequent bursting (mostly about the middle of the barrel) seems to prove that it was so. They might fire quicker than we did, but such hurried firing scarcely admits of precision.'[43]

Conical touch-holes, however, like those on Prussian muskets, permitted powder to be forced safely into the priming-pan from the barrel by the action of ramming the charge, obviating the separate filling of the pan. William Müller was among advocates of this system in his attempts to establish a system of platoon-firing which would permit the rate of fire to rise even in excess of the five rounds per minute claimed by Prussia. Although such abbreviations of the firing-drill could increase the rate of fire, it was probably not of great consequence in action, three rounds per minute probably being the most practical rate. The Duke of York sanctioned trials in 1802 and 1805 to test foreign drill against British, but against the Prussian claim of five rounds per minute the best attained in 1802 was three rounds in forty-nine seconds and five in ninety seconds. Tests undertaken in America by William Duane managed eighteen shots in five minutes, thirty-six in thirteen minutes, a logical slowing after the initial quick burst, and the rate would decrease more markedly as the barrels became too hot to handle. (Duane also noted no marked difference between an unencumbered man and one wearing full kit.) In combat, however, while a brief burst of rapid fire might be crucial on occasion, it could not be sustained as muskets became choked with burned powder, flints deteriorated, and the target became obscured by gun smoke. An Austrian commentator remarked on the importance of soldiers being able to fire rapidly – four shots per minute – but said that under normal campaign circumstances such speed could be disadvantageous, both from the rapid consumption of ammunition and uncertainty of resupply, and the fact that such rapid fire was unduly tiring for the musketeer. To emphasise the need to conserve ammunition, he noted that if a unit fired at four shots per minute, after only a quarter of an hour they would have expended all the cartridges normally carried and would be reduced to defending themselves with bayonets.

Effectiveness, rather than speed, was what was most required, as advocated by Suvarov's maxim, 'Fire seldom but fire sure', or as another commentator remarked, 'cool and deliberate and continuous discharge',[44] with French witnesses describing how it was the quick but steady fire of the

British that was truly insupportable. John Mitchell was more forthright: 'Tacticians talk, no doubt, about firing four and five shots in a minute. Miserable puerilities, not worth discussing. With ball cartridges three shots may perhaps be *fired*, but the more there is of such fire, the less will be the effect produced.'[45] Such opinions seem confirmed by accounts of what actually happened; for example, James Anton remarked of Quatre Bras: 'We had wasted a deal of ammunition this day, and surely to very little effect ... our commanding officer cautioned us against this useless expenditure of ammunition, and we became a little more economical.'[46]

Calculations about the effectiveness of musketry that derive from battlefield experience are difficult to assess without knowledge of the range at which fire was opened; this could be as diverse as the Spanish at Talavera discouraging French cavalry by volley-fire at 1,000 yards (914 metres), to accounts which tell of the exchange of volleys at ten yards (nine metres). It is often difficult to deduce precise ranges from eyewitness accounts, and there is sometimes much confusion (perhaps best exemplified, albeit from another war, by the 'Thin Red Line' of the 93rd Highlanders at Balaclava, where instead of the popular perception of Robert Gibb's famous painting, which has the Russians almost falling upon the line's bayonets, their musketry seems to have been delivered at extreme range and caused very few casualties). Contemporary comments can also be misleading; for example, to British witnesses accustomed to reserving their fire for short range, other practices seemed illogical. Thomas Austin remarked that the Prussians customarily opened fire at too long a range, 'resulting in a great waste of ammunition, and the loss of energy too soon expended, and which does not possess one countervailing advantage. I have seen Austrian troops commence firing with old flint muskets at an enemy six or seven hundred yards distance from them.'[47]

Some held that opening fire at long range was a sign of unsteady troops: certain British observers, for example, commented unfavourably upon the Spanish for wasting ammunition in this way, but this overlooked the fact that it was advocated by the Spanish regulations, which ordered infantry to commence firing during an advance perhaps as far as 600 paces from the enemy; presumably this was intended to unsettle the enemy's nerve much as did the skirmish-fire of other armies. (Evidently it could be counter-productive, as Wellington reported of his allies: 'Nearly 2,000 ran off on the evening of the 27th from the battle of Talavera ... who were neither attacked, nor threatened with an attack, and who were frightened only by the noise of their own

fire: they left their arms and accoutrements on the ground, and their officers went with them.'[48]) Napoleon himself remarked that he believed that
infantry, when attacked by cavalry, should fire at a distance and not reserve
their musketry for close range; but though he evidently explained his rea-
soning, Las Cases (who recorded the conversation) appears not to have
taken it down.[49]

Conversely, a common belief was that fire should be reserved until the
enemy was at close range; as Humphrey Bland had written in 1727, 'It is a
received maxim, that those who preserve their fire the longest, will be sure
to conquer.'[50] In practice, however, it seems that troops frequently opened
fire too soon, at longer range, for the problem of maintaining fire-discipline
was especially remarked upon. Some commentators blamed junior officers
for opening fire too early, but noted that once it had commenced, the men
tended to blaze away almost independently, frustrating all attempts to make
then cease. This must have been caused by the stress of battle, as suggested by a story recounted by John Kincaid, who at Ciudad Rodrigo asked a
rifleman who was shooting aimlessly, 'What, sir, are you firing at?'; 'I don't
know, sir! I am firing because everybody else is!'[51] Such was the problem of
unauthorised firing that as late as 1799 an experienced officer advocated a
return to the old plug-bayonet, which when 'fixed' made it impossible to
fire, as a way of implementing fire-discipline: 'by which means you become
master of the men's fire; you will never be so without it'.[52] Various means
were used to impose fire-discipline; a use of the legendary exhortation was
actually recorded in skirmishing near Bayonne, when the commander of the
assembled light companies of Hill's Corps called to his men when confronted by advancing French skirmishers, 'Dinna fire, men, till ye see the
wheights of their eyes.'[53] A more robust exclamation was recorded by
Roderick Murchison of the British 36th who recalled at Vimeiro 'old Burne
(our Colonel) crying, as he shook his yellow cane, that he would "knock
down any man who fired a shot!"'[54] More practical was to give the men a
mark at which to aim: at Mandora, for example, Daniel Nicol noted that as
the French advanced: 'Our commanding officer ordered us not to fire but to
stand firm until we could see their feet as they advanced from the hollow in
front of us.'[55] Indeed, fire-discipline was probably at least as important as the
ability to deliver musketry with proficiency, in order to maximise its effect;
one of the reasons for the success of the British system of repelling attacks
seems to have been the ability to hold fire until the enemy had approached
within close range.

Firing was often conducted in volleys, which could be delivered in a number of ways: by a massed discharge from an entire line, by platoons (so that musketry would be issuing from some part of a line at all times), by ranks or 'file-firing', with a volley beginning at one end of a line and running along it, and with fire once commenced allowing the men to fire at their own time. In all systems except the massed discharge, some men would always be ready to fire while their comrades were reloading, most useful when beating off successive waves of cavalry, for example. Another factor, commented on by the Marquis de Silva in 1768 for example, was that firing by platoon or general volley could be less effective than firing by ranks, for when two or three ranks fired together some of the enemy would be hit by more than one ball, and would thus protect those behind them; whereas if one rank fired, the casualties thus caused would fall and open the ranks behind them to the subsequent fire of the second rank.

It was also suggested that the accuracy of musketry might have been affected by the nature of the command to commence volley-firing. Subsequent to the Napoleonic Wars British drill dispensed with the order 'Fire!' but allowed each man to shoot in his own time once he had levelled his musket, though this was not to allow the soldier time to aim: 'Individual aim in volley-firing, in close order, it is absurd to expect, nor is it necessary: a good level is all that can be required. Volleys are used against large bodies, not against individual small objects.'[56] Without a command, however, it was thought that men might be so concerned to fire at the same moment as their fellows that they might shoot before having levelled the musket. Prussian tests found that volleys were generally more effective when a full sequence of commands was given ('Ready!' – 'Aim!' – 'Fire!') than with just the order 'Fire!' or with no command at all, though in some cases more accuracy was obtained without any command than with just 'Fire!', presumably because if left to their own time most men would level properly before pulling the trigger.

Further waste of shot occurred when young or unsteady troops fired wildly, often in the air. There are several accounts of this – for example, some from Waterloo – and it was probably taken as an indication that the troops were unreliable. This, incidentally, was not a universal opinion regarding such behaviour: for example, when in Afghanistan in 1880 the 30th Bombay Native Infantry (Jacob's Rifles) was observed firing wildly in this manner, their colonel thought it not the unsteadiness of fear but simply a reaction of young soldiers on going into action for the first time;

though the unit did subsequently break at Maiwand.[57] Such a view may, in fact, be one reason for so many accounts of volleys passing over the heads of the target.

Another factor in assessing the effectiveness of musketry, as Clausewitz commented, was the formation of the target: when firing against a solid phalanx of men most shots might be expected to take effect at close range, whereas when firing against a line of skirmishers many shots would pass between the gaps. The same proposition would be valid if an outnumbered unit extended its line to match that of the enemy, creating gaps in its own line, which Clausewitz stated was a common occurrence.

The effect of a single volley, delivered at close range, could be devastating, though it may be significant that volleys of great destruction were especially remarked upon, suggesting that they might not have been common. One was witnessed at Sabugal, when French cavalry rode up to a wall and

Treatises on the efficiency of weaponry and the technique of war cannot conceal the essential tragedy which was the ultimate result, powerfully expressed in this scene of a mortally wounded French NCO. (Print after Hippolyte Bellangé.)

were firing their pistols over it when British infantry, presumably unseen by them, shot them nearly all with one volley. Another squadron suffered similarly at Orthez when riding up a lane, and was shot down by infantry from behind an overhanging bank. Yet another was witnessed at Waterloo, when a retiring body of French cuirassiers was stopped by a roadblock on the Nivelles road and received a volley from the British 51st, from which it was said only one Frenchman escaped. William Wheeler, an experienced soldier, went to see the effect of the volley and remarked that he had 'never before beheld such a sight in as short a space'.[58] William Lawrence saw another terrible volley in the Peninsula, which was in return for one delivered first by the French: 'I never saw a single volley do so much execution in all my campaigning days, almost every man of their first two ranks falling; and then we instantly charged and chased them down the mountain, doing still further and more fearful havoc.'[59]

Alternatively, there are accounts of musketry doing remarkably little damage, as at Waterloo where 'the few that fell by the fire of the squares was ... a matter of great astonishment'.[60] Contemporary accounts can be deceptive, as in the case of the protracted firefight at Barouillet on 12 December 1813. Here, a strong French force kept up an interchange of fire for as long as three hours, from under cover and at about 100 yards' (91 metres) range, upon two brigades of British Foot Guards and a detachment of 5/60th Royal Americans. The fusillade was described by one officer as 'tremendous',[61] yet the total British casualties were 28 killed and 164 wounded, which can hardly have represented more than five per cent of the numbers engaged, surely many fewer than might have been expected after such an expenditure of shot at close range.

In protracted firefights, however, like Albuera, the slaughter could be appalling. Under such conditions, when it must be surprising that men would stand, in the open, and exchange shots over a long period, it must be likely that instead of disciplined musketry, order and control would have broken down very considerably. John Mitchell gave an example of what could happen:

What precision of aim or direction can be expected from soldiers when firing in line? One man is priming; another is coming to the present; a third is taking, what is called, aim; a fourth is ramming down his cartridge. After the first few shots the entire body are [*sic*] closely enveloped in smoke, so that the enemy is totally invisible;

some of the soldiers step out a pace or two, in order to get a better shot; others kneel down; and some have no objection to retreat a step or so. The doomed begin to fall, dreadfully mutilated perhaps, and even bold men shrink from the sight; others are wounded, and assisted to the rear by their comrades; so that the whole soon becomes a line of utter confusion, in which the mass only think of getting their shot fired, they hardly care how or in what direction. True it is that, owing to the crowding in on some points, and casualties on others, elbow-room is sometimes got fast enough; but by that time the blood is already rushing with lightning speed and fire through the veins, excitement is at its height; all composure is out of the question; and your well-drilled battalion is fit for little more than a dash to the front, or a flight to the rear, and totally unfit to withstand the least shock or onset made with efficient arms – unable also to make any very skilful use of the musket, which to be rendered effective must be used with a certain degree of coolness and composure.[63]

The flash of a musket could set alight anything it touched, even soldiers' clothing (and in 1811 about twenty-four cottages in the village of Merriott, near Crewkerne, were destroyed when thatched roofing was set alight by a man shooting rats). A terrible consequence of this was the ignition of dry grass on the battlefield, which might burn any helpless wounded, as occurred at Talavera: 'Standing corn & high stubble ... was set in a blaze several times during the day, & Lines of running fire half a mile in length were frequent & fatal to many a Soldier, some by their pouches blowing up in passing the fire, other Wounded unable to reach their respective Armies lying weltering in their gore with the devouring element approaching & death most horrid staring them in the face!'[64] George Wood remarked that the bodies looked like roasted pigs, and that French casualties could be distinguished 'only by their ear-rings ... with their clothes entirely consumed'.[65] Blazing wheat-fields which ignited cartridge-boxes even caused French troops to retreat at Marengo, such was the danger.

A further consequence of protracted musketry was the 'fog of war', the immense cloud of gun smoke which settled over a battlefield, often reducing visibility to a very few yards. It could be truly impenetrable: at the end of the Battle of Waterloo, for example, Harry Smith recalled that he realised someone had been beaten when the firing slackened, but he had no idea who, so that 'this was the most anxious moment of my life',[66] anxiety only

Right:
Top, Girardoni air rifle, the Austrian Repetier-Windbüchse of 1780. The 20-shot magazine could be fired in less than half a minute, propelled by compressed air held in a reservoir in the butt. This held sufficient for 30 shots, but the pressure dropped as the reservoir emptied so that range declined markedly towards the end of the supply. It required from five to ten minutes' pumping to replenish the reservoir. Calibre 13mm, length 122cm. (Print after R. von Ottenfeld.) Bottom, Crespi breech-loading carbine; calibre 18.3mm, length 123cm (48.4in). Issued originally to the Austrian cavalry, Crespi breech-loaders were later carried by Austrian volunteer corps. The design, including the spear-bayonet, was copied by Durs Egg and issued as a trial to some British regiments in 1788. The bayonet when not 'fixed' was reversed and carried under the barrel with the blade in a clip at the front of the trigger-guard. (Print after R. von Ottenfeld.)

dispelled when a momentary break in the smoke showed the enemy retiring. The smoke could entirely conceal the movements of the enemy, as Dawson Kelly observed of Waterloo: 'The fog and smoke lay so heavy upon the ground that we could only ascertain the approach of the Enemy by the noise and clashing of arms which the French usually make in their advance', from which, he thought, accounts of battles which purported to be accurate 'must have a good deal of fancy in the narrative'.[67] Even when the smoke was not completely dense, it was sufficient to conceal the identity of troops even nearby (hence much of the confusion which occurred in battle, troops even attacking their own side by mistake). Charles James Napier, for example, remarked of Busaco that although he was only 300 yards away, no one could distinguish whether the 88th, which was nearest to them, was a British regiment dressed in red, or a Portuguese in blue!

As noted before, sustained musketry could soon exhaust a soldier's supply of ammunition, even though in the field many soldiers crammed more cartridges into their pockets, in extra cartridge-boxes or even into their headdress, and where possible ammunition would be resupplied during a battle. When it ran out entirely, however, there are accounts of soldiers pelting their opponents with stones: instances include Alexandria, where the British 28th and their French opponents both ran out of ammunition and began to hurl stones; at La Haye Sainte; in the Pyrenees; and at Garcia Hernandez, where Foy's infantry tried to repel cavalry with a barrage of stones (although conceivably this involved men who had dropped their muskets in earlier flight and had re-formed). The throwing of stones was not always an act of desperation, however: a story was recounted of Lieutenant

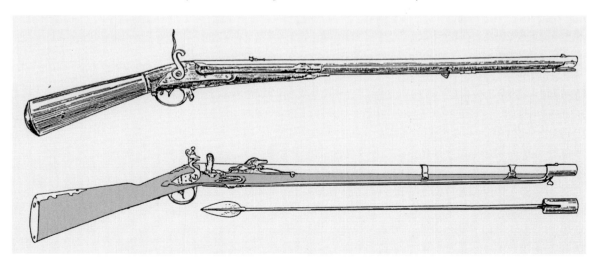

William Irwin of the British 28th, who captured seven or eight Frenchmen in the Peninsula by throwing rocks at them. He dropped two with such accuracy that the remainder surrendered!

RIFLES

Despite their potential for greater accuracy, rifled muskets were not used widely, to some extent because in the prevailing system of war it was not necessary to hit an individual at a distance. Rifles operated with the same mechanism as the smooth-bored musket, except that the internal rifling of the barrel imparted a spin to the ball, thus enhancing its accuracy. The projectile was the same spherical ball as used with the smooth-bore, even though as early as 1747 Benjamin Robins had suggested that bullets of 'an egg-like form' would be more accurate. Scharnhorst also experimented with ovoid bullets fired from a smoothbore, but they compared rather unfavourably with shooting by a rifle.

In addition to the rifled barrel, other technological developments had been made but were of limited consequence. Breech-loading weapons had been used only fleetingly, perhaps most notably in the rifle designed by Patrick Ferguson and used by his own small unit in the War of American Independence. It was certainly a superior weapon, combining great accuracy with rapidity of fire (in a trial Ferguson himself averaged four shots per minute while advancing at four miles an hour, and fired six shots in one minute), but it appears that, especially in dry, warm conditions, it was prone to excessive fouling, so that loading was difficult and effectiveness declined markedly. The British also experimented with breech-loading carbines in the 1780s, produced by the gunsmith Durs Egg, but beyond a trial issue the project was not taken up. Egg's pattern was based upon that designed by Giuseppe Crespi of Milan, whose breechloaders had been used by the Austrian cavalry but had been discontinued for not being gas-tight, although they were carried by some Austrian

Above: A member of the University Brigade of the Vienna Volunteers, 1797, armed with the Crespi breech-loader with its distinctive spear-bayonet. (Print after Jacquemin.)

Above: Austrian Jäger wearing the 1798 helmet; note the long socket-bayonet for use with the short rifle. (Print after R. von Ottenfeld.)

Above right: Austrian Jäger, 1809; his powder-horn is suspended from cords over the shoulder. (Print after R. von Ottenfeld.)

auxiliary formations during the early Napoleonic period. In America, John H. Hall patented his breech-loading rifle in 1811, but although military trials were conducted it was not adopted by the US Army until after the War of 1812. A further technological development was the 1779 Girardoni air rifle, a 20-shot repeater issued to Austrian *Jägers* in 1792–7 and 1799, but difficulty of maintenance in the field led to its withdrawal in 1800, although it remained in official stores until 1815.

As early as 1747 Benjamin Robins had remarked that whichever state perfected a military rifle and trained its troops accordingly would produce results little short of the effect on warfare of the first use of gunpowder; but nevertheless the issue of rifles remained very limited, as did the production of official patterns, at least when compared to the huge quantities of smoothbores which were manufactured. Indeed, on occasion no attempt was even made to provide a standard rifle; for example, when Saxony

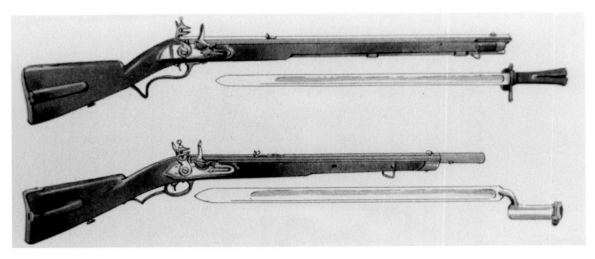

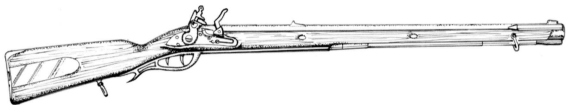

formed a *Jäger* corps in 1809, it was the result of an appeal for volunteers from experienced huntsmen who were to bring their own rifles to the army, and this was not an isolated case. Certain regions had a long tradition of rifleshooting, which provided a supply of experienced marksmen for the Austrian and some German armies in particular (it is noteworthy that one of the British Army's most famous rifle corps, the 5th Battalion, 60th Royal Americans, was originally largely German in composition). Rifle-armed troops had been deployed by armies such as these earlier in the eighteenth century, but although of considerable significance in skirmishing, their effect can be overestimated. For example, despite the reputation of American riflemen, the use of rifles during the War of Independence was very restricted when compared to the number of smoothbores used, and even at New Orleans there appear to have been only small numbers of rifle-men in the US force.

In addition to the regular *Jäger* corps, Austria deployed rifle-armed troops in the early *Frei-Corps* and *Grenz* (border) units, and until the loss of that territory in 1805 had the benefit of calling upon the inhabitants of the Tyrol, of whom one commentator remarked 'The fondness of the Tyrolese for shooting amounts to a complete passion.'[69] (Originally Regt. No. 46,

Above: Prussian Model 1810 Jäger rifle (sometimes styled the Neue-Corpsbüchse); calibre 14.7mm, barrel-length 73cm. Some rifles, as in this case, had two triggers, one needing only a very light touch to fire, as an aid to accurate shooting.

Above left: Austrian Jäger rifles. Top: pattern of 1779, calibre 17.6mm, overall length 110cm (43.3in), brass fittings, with Hirschfänger-style sword-bayonet. Bottom: pattern of 1795, calibre 14.5mm, overall length 105.2cm (41.4in), brass fittings, with socket-hilted sword-bayonet. (Print after R. von Ottenfeld.)

styled *Tiroler Land- und Feld-Regiment*, included a rifle battalion, and in 1803 a *Tiroler-Jäger-Regiment* was formed as no. 64 in the line.) The regulation *Jäger* rifles were the models of 1779 (calibre 17.6mm), 1795 (14.5mm) and 1807 (13.9mm), but the *Grenzers* had carried a more unusual weapon, the 1768 and 1795 *Doppelstutz* of 14.8mm calibre. This had one rifled and one smoothbore barrel, with a lock on each side of the stock, and was used with a short pike or *Hackenlanze* ('hook lance') which as the name suggests had an adjustable hook to act as a support for the gun-barrels, in the style of the seventeenth-century musket-rest.

Similarly, the Prussians used a variety of rifled weapons, many foresters and gamekeepers bringing their own weapons with them when they joined the army, though attempts were made to standardise in 1796 and in 1810, when the 'New Corps' *Jägerbüchse* was introduced (known also as the 'Potsdam rifle'), of 14.6mm calibre, but its use never became universal and various other rifles continued in service. There was also an 18.5mm 'sharpshooter' rifle of 1787 (*Schützengewehr*) carried by the *Schützen* (sharpshooter) detachments of infantry units. Similarly, Russian *Jäger* regiments also carried a variety of weapons, but although some 20,000 Tula rifles were issued between 1803 and 1812, they were carried only by NCOs and designated marksmen, the remainder using ordinary muskets.

One of the most famous rifles of the period was the British regulation weapon designed by Ezekiel Baker (though the first 'regulation' rifle was probably that commissioned from Durs Egg in 1796). The Baker existed in a number of varieties, with calibres varying from 0.615 to 0.7 inches (usually 6.25 inches, carbine-bore), although most other differences were in minor details of fittings such as the presence of a patch-box in the butt or the introduction of a reinforced cock. More than 30,000 of the Baker were produced between 1800 and 1815, equipping not only the regular rifle corps (95th Foot, the rifle-armed battalions of the 60th, the light battalions of the King's German Legion and a few rifle companies of other regiments) but also auxiliary units (including militia and volunteers) and allied formations like the Portuguese *Caçadores*. The first regiment to be entirely armed with rifles

Right: French rifle of An XII pattern, the 1793 Carabine de Versailles with a ring-neck or reinforced cock; hexagonal barrel 65cm long.

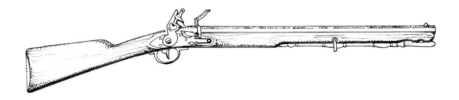

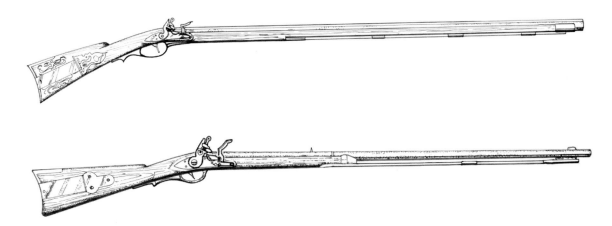

was the 95th, formed in 1800 as the 'Experimental Corps of Riflemen' as a training unit from which men were intended to be sent to instruct rifle sections in line regiments, but following deployment at Ferrol they were taken on to the establishment as a complete regiment, which took the number 95 in the line.

It is perhaps somewhat odd that the most important army of the period, Napoleon's, had hardly any experience with the rifle. Some rifled weapons were used before the Revolution (the 1781 *carabine*), and both infantry and cavalry rifles were produced in 1793, the so-called '*Carabine de Versailles*' (from the place of manufacture). Like most rifles it had a short barrel (65cm; 25.6in) which was hexagonal in section, with a calibre of 13.5mm. It was not a success, being difficult to load and originally not taking a bayonet, and although the great gunmaker Nicolas Boutet produced an improved version, the '*An XII*' rifles, of which a couple of thousand were manufactured, they were still not successful although ordered to be distributed among officers and sergeants of *voltigeurs*. It was not popular and it is doubtful how many were actually used, even though it was up to twelve times more accurate than the ordinary musket.

Also worthy of note is the Pennsylvania or Kentucky rifle encountered in America, derived from European *Jäger* rifles and produced initially by immigrant gunsmiths. Often having a somewhat angled butt and elaborate decoration, in the hands of a skilled marksman it was most effective: as one of its opponents remarked, it 'made some *noise* in the world, and done *quite* a mint of mischief'.[70] Such weapons were essentially private firearms, and while doubtless used by militia and similar formations, the official US rifle used in the War of 1812 was the Model 1803, manufactured at Harper's

Top: Pennsylvania or Kentucky rifle, as used in America, usually by irregular troops. The curved butt, long and fully stocked barrel and the elaborate metalwork around the hinged patch-box in the butt were all typical of this renowned weapon.

Above: *US Harpers Ferry rifle, Model 1803, the first US government-manufactured rifle. Calibre .54in, barrel length 33in (83.8cm), partly round and partly octagonal. Brass fittings (including large patch-box in the butt) but no provision for a bayonet.*

Ferry, with calibre 0.54in and only half-stocked; the succeeding Model 1807 (which did not supplant the 1803, manufacture of which recommenced in 1814) was fully stocked. The Model 1803 was probably the rifle carried by the regular army's single Regiment of Riflemen, formed in 1808.

The rifled barrel not only increased accuracy by imparting a spin to the ball, but when loaded with a greased patch around the ball (which might be kept in a lidded 'patch-box' in the butt) made the ball fit more tightly and thus reduced 'windage'. It also served to make the loading of a rifle much slower than that of a smoothbore, the fit being so tight that sometimes the ball had to be driven down the barrel using the ramrod and a hammer. (Ezekiel Baker noted that when he first equipped the British 95th he provided wooden mallets for this purpose, but not surprisingly they were found 'very inconvenient' and were soon discarded). Powder could be used 'loose', from a powder-horn (sometimes with a separate small flask of more finely ground priming-powder), which one officer claimed increased accuracy, as an experienced rifleman could thereby gauge the most effective charge, minimising recoil by not using too great a charge for the task in hand. The rifling also became more easily fouled with burned powder, making loading even more difficult, and reducing the efficiency of the grooves which imparted the spin; it was observed that after only twenty-five shots in dry weather the accuracy began to deteriorate. For this reason it was remarked especially of the Austrian *Jägers* that they never threw away shots on chance, but made every one tell, in the knowledge that each successive shot tended to diminish accuracy.

To increase the speed of fire, however, prepared cartridges with a ball of carbine-bore could be used instead of separate balls and loose powder. With this load the Baker rifle, for example, could match the rate of fire of a musket, so that troops thus armed could play the role of line infantry if necessary. This was especially observed of the 95th's defence of the bridge at Barba del Puerco in March 1810, when they repelled a French attack unaided, which led the commander of the Light Division, Robert Craufurd, to remark: 'In other armies the rifle is considered ill-calculated for close action with an enemy armed with musket and bayonet: but the 95th Regiment has proven that the rifle in the hands of a British soldier is a fully sufficient weapon to enable him to defeat the French in the closest fight',[71] perhaps the first time this had been demonstrated so clearly.

The relative slowness of rifle-fire led to the practice in some armies of issuing rifles to only a part of a unit, as with the Russian *Jägers*, for example.

In Austrian service, when NCOs and one-third of the privates carried rifles, the remainder were armed with carbines: the 1807 carbine, for example, was longer than the equivalent rifle (123cm to 105.2cm; 48.4in to 41.4in), smoothbored, and of musket-bore. The intention was for the rifle-armed men to form a third rank when acting in line, and to be deployed as skirmishers when required, when the carbine-armed first two ranks would act as their reserve, so that the faster carbine-fire and more deliberate rifle-fire combined the best aspects of both weapons within the same unit. Similarly, rifles might be carried by only a few members of a unit otherwise armed with smoothbores: examples included a plan by the Archduke Charles to arm selected infantrymen with rifles to enhance their skirmishing ability, the attachment of volunteer *Jäger* companies to Prussian regiments during the 'War of Liberation', and even the use of a few rifles by French *voltigeurs* prior to about 1809. At various times during the period a few British regiments maintained rifle-armed detachments, and rifles might even be carried unofficially by individuals: Ensign Joseph Owgan of the British 88th in the Peninsula, for example, had a reputation as a dead shot with the rifle he carried in action.

The short barrel of the rifle made loading easier than the musket in kneeling and prone positions, especially when riflemen were expected to take advantage of the smallest cover. Among postures adopted for rifle-shooting was that used by the British marksman Tom Plunket[72] when he killed General Auguste de Colbert at Cacabellos: 'To fire laying [*sic*] on the back, the sling must be sufficiently loosened to let it be passed on the ball of the right foot, and as the leg is kept stiff, so, on the contrary, the butt is pulled towards the breast, the head is raised up, till the front sight is brought into the notch in the usual way ... the position is not only awkward but painful.'[73]

Training a rifleman took longer than for a musketeer, for as one commentator remarked, skill in rifle-shooting involved not only steadiness of eye and hand but also the ability to judge distance, the influence of sun and atmosphere on that ability, and the effect of wind and the nature of the ground over which the ball passed, all of which could only be attained by experience. Very considerable feats could be achieved with a rifle. With one of his own rifles, Ezekiel Baker

Below: Some irregular forces placed more emphasis on target-practice than did most regular units, in the expectation that many irregulars would have been of most value serving as skirmishers. This medal for target-shooting is typical, awarded by Capt. Francis Astley of the Dukinfield Independent Riflemen in 1805, a corps formed in the previous year and associated with the Manchester Rifle Regiment.

fired at a man-sized target, 34 shots at 100 yards (91 metres) and 24 at 200 yards (183 metres) and *every one* hit. Scharnhorst's trials involved only Prussian and Russian weapons, and although some of his shooters were not familiar with rifles, against a target 6 feet high by 4 feet wide (1.82 x 1.22 metres) the weapons registered 68–69 per cent hits at 150 paces 49 per cent at 200, and 24–31 per cent at 300, though accuracy fell off markedly when cartridges rather than ball and patch were used. The rate of fire varied between one and three shots per minute (much faster with cartridges), and the rifle proved four times more accurate than a smoothbore at longer range.

Some complained that riflemen were taught to fire at too short a range:

For, say they, a rifle should begin where a musket ceases to be of use; and, unless riflemen are kept at least 250 yards from a line of musketry, the latter will, by their greater facility and expedition in loading and firing, drive the former out of the field ... but, as the most powerful inducement to the adoption of longer ranges ... we only wish to recall to mind, that from a musket at 300 yards, not one shot in 100, or rather we may say 300, would, if fired at a *single* man as the object, take effect; when on the contrary, with a rifle, we may take, at the least, one in five; but more likely, in skilful hands, one in three as a fair average.[74]

Above: Although not needed when prepared cartridges were used, the powder-horn or flask was an important part of a rifleman's equipment: this typical example was carried by the Percy Tenantry Volunteers, a Northumberland rifle corps.

Rapidity of fire was generally less important than its effectiveness, a point made by a member of what became the British Light Division, who recorded a comparison between rifle and musket which occurred shortly before their departure for the Peninsula. He remarked that although it took longer to load a rifle, 'in ninety-nine cases out of a hundred, *two* rifle shots shall cause more death and destruction than *three* or *four* discharges from a musket, allowing both the rifleman and the light bob to be tolerably fair artists in their way' (this obviously did not relate to ordinary musketry, but to the *aimed* fire from smoothbores practised by trained light infantry). A rifleman, he stated, 'should by no means attempt to keep up the same random, and too often, ineffectual fire, which I have often witnessed by light companies'; but if instead 'he takes proper advantage of the weapon he bears, and expends few shots without either *actually hitting* or *going very near his pursuers*, nothing will so much tend to make them keep at a respectable distance, or to cool their ardour. I know of nothing that makes skirmishers mind their business more than being actually opposed to a scattered line of good marksmen.' He recorded a session of target-practice between a light infantry company and a rifle company, each about eighty strong. '*Six rounds* had been fired by every man of both parties; the rifle company having its target placed at *two hundred* yards (the usual distance) and the light infantry company at between eighty and ninety yards. The *contingent allowance* of the rifle captain suffered severely on that occasion, as the target was so riddled and cut to pieces, that it was with difficulty brought home; whilst the target of the light infantry was, comparatively, in a good state of repair.'[75] He added that attempts by the 95th Rifles to practise against moving targets, dragged along the beach at Hythe, were frustrated by the shots repeatedly cutting the dragging ropes to pieces!

Effectiveness in combat was probably not so marked, although there are many accounts of remarkable feats, and an experienced marksman could wreak real havoc in favourable circumstances. The aforementioned Thomas Plunket, for example, was especially distinguished at Buenos Ayres, where he was hoisted on to a roof from where he fired for some hours. When asked later about what he had accomplished, he said 'I think I killed about twenty, Sir: I shot a gentleman with a flag of truce, Sir!'[76] Not surprisingly, members of rifle corps tended to praise their own weapons and the skill with which they were used; Surtees, for example, believed that

The equipment of a rifleman exemplified in this study of a member of the North York Militia: in this case the powder-flask is somewhat unusually carried in a pocket on the breast of the jacket. In the background a rifleman is using his shako as a rest for the barrel of his rifle, apparently quite a common practice. (Print after George Walker.)

on average one rifle-shot in twenty took effect. Others were less sure. G. B. Jackson, for example, was one of those who thought that the light infantry musket was just as effective as a rifle in action, and other comparisons were made involving American marksmen. Surtees thought that they understood the science of shooting better than the British, and John Mitchell agreed that individually they were immeasurably more skilled in the handling of firearms, 'and, as brave men, they naturally made the most of the advantage'. Nevertheless, he believed that under combat conditions the prowess of riflemen was exaggerated, for 'in all the actions fought on open ground, where the fire of both parties could tell, the fire of the common English shots invariably produced a greater effect than that of the most skilful Americans',[77] which presumably relates not to the accuracy of individual weapons but to the greater volume of fire which could be delivered by the ordinary musket.

The ability of a rifle to hit an individual at a considerable distance raised a question concerning the morality of war. Although it was good sense to take down the enemy's officers and NCOs, which was done without hesitation by riflemen, it is likely that there was disapproval on the part of other soldiers, as being contrary to the spirit of the 'rules of war'. Moyle Sherer heard two British soldiers mourning the death of a brave French officer: '"I was sorry to see him drop, poor fellow," said one. "Ah!" said another, "He came so close there was no missing him; I did for him!" "Did you!" rejoined the first speaker; "By God, I could not have pulled a trigger at him. No; damn me, I like fair fighting and hot fighting; but I could not single out such a man in cold blood."'[78] As late as 1839 it was remarked that the sharpshooter who had shot Horatio Nelson had deliberately aimed at him with 'detestable pertinacity', evidence that 'the French were ahead of us in cunning means and appliances to destroy life', whereas in the British fleet no order was ever given to single out an enemy officer, 'from a too generous and noble motive'![79] Given the sharpshooting abilities of British riflemen this hardly seems fair, and most skirmishers would have had sympathy with the German rifleman observed by George Landmann at Vimeiro, deliberately aiming at a French officer in the expectation that his body would yield more plunder than if he had shot a common soldier instead! Nevertheless, there is evidence that sharpshooters were not appreciated by some ordinary infantrymen: for example, the nickname given to the Austrian *Jägers*, 'Grey Devils', may be significant, and when La Haye Sainte was captured, two wounded riflemen were killed by the French who declared, 'No quarter for these green *coquins*', per-haps evidence that they regarded sharpshooters in general as a type of assassin.

BAYONETS

All muskets, and the majority of rifles, were provided with a bayonet, the utility of which aroused much heated discussion in the years following the Napoleonic Wars. John Kincaid stated that the bayonet was 'wedded to the musket as much as a man is to his wife, and they are sharers alike in glory or disgrace, for the one would be imperfect without the other. It goes for nothing that the musket usually takes the greater share of the duty; for if men prefer standing to shoot, and standing to be shot, in place of walking up and running each other through the body, it is a mere matter of taste, and furnishes no ground for argument against the bayonet.'[80]

The original design of the weapon was known as a 'plug-bayonet': it resembled a knife, the handle of which was thrust into the muzzle of the musket, making firing impossible. It was clearly an imperfect design, and was supplanted by the socket-bayonet, in which the blade (usually triangular in section) was set off-centre upon a tubular iron socket which slipped over the muzzle and was held in place initially only by the front sight. Nevertheless, the manufacture of plug-bayonets continued, notably in Spain: even though the socket-bayonet had come into military use there by

Right: German rifles were often equipped with sword-bayonets, such as this Prussian example with brass hilt, though a number of varieties existed. They were sometimes termed as a Hirschfänger, lit. 'deer-hunter', emphasising their similarity with hunting-knives which may have been their origin.

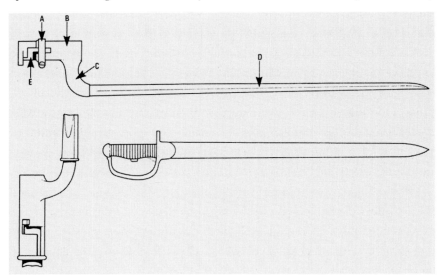

Left: Bayonets. Top: typical bayonet with triangular-sectioned blade, with parts identified. Key: (A) locking ring, (B) socket, (C) shoulder or 'bend of the shank', (D) blade, (E) zigzag in socket. Bottom: left, British socket bayonet without locking ring, showing how the zigzag fitted over the front-sight of the musket; right, 2nd pattern sword-bayonet for the Baker rifle, the lug below the hand-grip operating the catch which attached it to the rifle.

the mid-eighteenth century, the plug-bayonet continued to be produced as a hunting tool even into the second half of the nineteenth century, and some plug-bayonets must surely have been used by irregulars during the Peninsular War. Some socket-bayonets, notably those of France (from as early as 1763) were equipped with a locking-ring to hold them in place on the muzzle, to prevent them being wrenched off in combat, being otherwise 'so badly fixed that the parry of even a briquet sends them on a journey to the moon'.[81] Nevertheless, the locking-ring was not present on many bayonets, for example those of the British Army (with a few exceptions: William Napier, for example, recalled that when Moore was training the 43rd and 52nd Light Infantry at Shorncliffe, he had bayonets issued which did have locking-rings). A much less common type of bayonet was a knife- or sword-like weapon with which some rifles were equipped (derived from the German *Hirschfänger* or hunting-sword), which clipped on to the side of the rifle and thus did not impair aiming by covering the front-sight (though a fixed bayonet did tend to unbalance the weapon).

A number of nations claimed the bayonet as their national weapon, as if to agree with Suvarov: 'Lead often misses, steel never; steel is a hero, lead is but a fool.'[82] Nevertheless, during the great 'bayonet debate' in the years subsequent to the Napoleonic Wars, some regarded the weapon as useless by virtue of the fact that in the open field, bayonet-fights were rare in the extreme. Among them was John Mitchell, who decried the bayonet as a 'rickety zigzag' of no use. Indeed, one officer somewhat facetiously listed its uses, such as when put into the keyhole of a door, it served as a guide to the place to shoot off the lock. 'A bayonet will also serve to prize [*sic*] up the lid of a box – it will tap a cask; when you are cooking cutlets across two ramrods *à la Tartare*, a couple of bayonets form excellent steak-tongs; stuck in the ground it makes a first-rate candlestick; it is a beautiful ornament to a barrack ball-room when collected into the shape of a star; and, finally, it forms a capital projectile, to shy at a fowl or duck in a farmyard.'[83] Undoubtedly the bayonet was used in all these ways on campaign, and it is also recorded as being fixed on a stick to form a short pike for use on foraging expeditions, when carrying a musket would be a burden. The heavy socket-end could be used as a club: John Cooper, for example, recalled how in the Peninsula he persuaded a reluctant cart-driver to take aboard some invalids: 'I drew my bayonet, took it by the small end, and swinging round, gave him such a blow on the mouth as stunned him. Then I got them into the car, and he drove on, holding his mouth as if he had got the *tic*.'[84]

Bayonets often seem to have been made of inferior metal, so that they broke or bent in use: a witness of a fight in South America observed 'some deficiency in the triangular shape of the bayonet; it would not penetrate between the ribs, and the weapon bent into the shape of a bow by the force; although, probably, the wounded men thought they had enough'.[85] Another recalled: 'I saw here, for the first time, the resistance a bayonet meets in passing through a man's ribs. One of our soldiers had his bayonet bent like a loop forcing it into a fellow's chest: it went far enough to do his business ...'[86] A similar story told how after the Battle of the Pyramids it was said that French troops were able to bend their bayonets into hooks with which to drag Mameluke bodies from the Nile in the hope of finding loot upon them.

In battle, however, bayonet wounds seem to have been very few. Exact casualty statistics are rarely available, but when the great French surgeon Dominique-Jean Larrey tried to ascertain the prevalence of bayonet-wounds in a close-quarter action by French and Austrian troops, his investigation suggested that only about four per cent of the wounds were inflicted by the bayonet.

Above: Close-quarter combat: Prussian Landwehr (right) storm a French position at Leipzig. (Print after F. de Myrbach.)

Even this is likely to have been a rather high figure for combat in general. Statistics are available for British casualties treated in field or general hospitals during the Crimean War (i.e. not including fatalities or the lightly wounded), but with some 1,815 casualties from the early part of the war unclassified, so that the figures will be somewhat distorted as the latter would include injuries from Inkerman and Balaclava, where hand-to-hand fighting did take place. Of the rest, there were only seventy-six bayonet-wounds (and eighty-seven sword or lance injuries) against 10,038 gunshot injuries, and presumably some of the few bayonet wounds were caused by accident (loading a musket with bayonet fixed could cause a laceration of the arm). Statistics for officers' wounds *are* comprehensive, and show ten bayonet injuries out of 579.[87] Even though the bayonet was probably less used than in the Napoleonic Wars, the statistics are striking.

Above: 'Charge Bayonets': the stance for delivering a bayonet-charge demonstrated by a member of the 3rd Loyal London Volunteers, 1804. (Print by Meyer & Lewis after James Green.)

John Mitchell stated: 'That in some scrambling attack of works, or hasty flight out of woods or villages, a soldier may, perhaps, have been killed or wounded with a bayonet is possible, but to suppose that soldiers ever rushed into close combat, armed only with bayonets, is an absurdity; it never happened and never can happen.'[88] Nevertheless, the Napoleonic Wars do provide plenty of examples of the use of the bayonet, sometimes in quite colourful terms, such as the member of the British 50th at Vimeiro who when asked why he was wiping his bayonet replied, 'By J——s, your Honour, I skiver'd three of 'em!'[89] Otherwise, bayonet-fights seem to have attracted an attention which suggests that they were rare occurrences.

For example, when the renowned Benjamin Harris was asked if he had ever seen a charge, he replied 'many'; but he had never seen bayonets cross, and so rare was the experience that after Vimeiro, 'I saw a soldier of the 43rd and a French grenadier lying both dead close together, apparently (I may say certainly) killed by thrusts of their bayonets. They appear to have met together with so much hatred, that they had killed each other at the same moment. Several of our Riflemen looked at these bodies with much curiosity', presumably because the sight was so rare.[90] (William Napier confirmed the story, and identified the 43rd man as Armourer-Sergeant Patrick). Similarly, in reporting the night attack before the Battle of New Orleans, General Gibbs noted that the contending parties were 'for some seconds hand to hand engaged, both officers and men ... a more extraordinary conflict never occurred',[91] and in describing a charge by the French 81st Line Regiment against a British naval landing-party at Grao, on the Gulf of Trieste, the comment was made that of the casualties, 'eight were bayonet wounds, which will convince you, sir, of the nature of the attack'.[92]

Certainly in the storm of defended places, or where troops encountered one another unexpectedly, bayonet-fights did occur, and there were some circumstances in which hand-to-hand fighting was the only practical course. An incident quoted as an example at the time occurred near Teitz in 1813, when the Saxon General Johann Thielmann (who by then had gone over to the Allies) attempted to capture a French strongpoint with a small force of hussars and cossacks. Having found gunfire quite ineffective, Thielmann's men rushed the place and captured it in the only way possible, by engaging the defenders at the closest quarters.

Much more on the efficacy of the bayonet as a psychological weapon is given in the section on infantry service, but despite the fact that it caused relatively few casualties, its value was summarised appropriately by William Napier:

> Men know, psychologically and physiologically, that whether it be called a 'rickety zigzag' or any other name, it will prick their flesh and let out life, and therefore they eschew it. Many persons will stand fire who will not stand a charge, and for this plain psychological reason – that there is great hope of escape in the first case, very little in the second, and hope is the great sustainer of courage. It is therefore not in the weapon, but in the man who bears it, that the harmlessness resides.[93]

SWORDS

Infantry swords fall into two categories: those carried by officers as a combination of (usually) their only weapon and a symbol of rank, and the short swords carried by other ranks in some armies; together with a few ornamental types carried by drum-majors and the like, and a few distinctive patterns carried by pioneers.

A common fashion was for officers' swords to be straight-bladed for 'battalion' or 'centre' companies, and for curved-bladed sabres to be carried by officers of 'élite' companies, light infantry and grenadiers, though the distinction was probably more a matter of tradition than utility. Sir John

Right:

1 *One of the most distinctive infantry swords was the basket-hilted broadsword carried by officers and some sergeants of Highland regiments. No regulation pattern was authorised until 1798 and many variations existed. This shows a not untypical basket-hilt, pierced with thistle motifs; it bears the engraved badge of the 1st Breadalbane Fencibles (raised 1793) but similar swords are known to have been used by the 116th Perthshire Highlanders, albeit with a different badge on the guard.*

Typical French officers' swords:
2 *Fusilier company épée with helmet-shaped pommel;*
3 *Sabre as favoured by officers of grenadiers and light infantry.*

Austrian officers' swords:
4 *Fusilier company épée;*
5 *Sabre of the type carried by officers of Hungarian regiments, 1811. Officers of Austrian grenadiers and light troops carried similar sabres, but generally with less ornate decoration.*

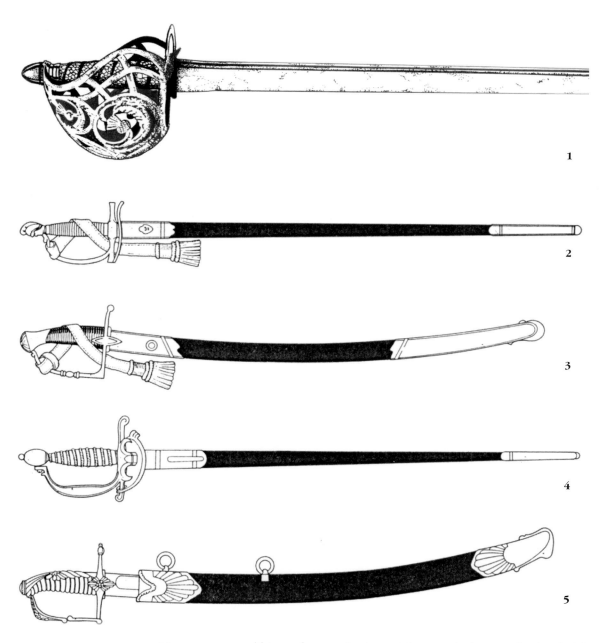

1

2

3

4

5

Moore expressed his preference for 'a straight sword, sharp on both edges' as being the most useful weapon, remarking that one had saved his life in Corsica, when he was attacked by a French grenadier with a bayonet. 'Moore, seeing his only chance of life was to run his sword through the man, he did so and killed him on the spot; now if he had not had a *straight* sword, but a sabre, he would not have been able to run the grenadier through the body, and would have been killed himself ... [but] he told me he should never forget the horrid sensation it gave him when drawing the sword out of the man's body, and that it was always a painful recollection to him.'[94]

British officers initially carried the straight-bladed 'spadroon' pattern authorised in 1786, succeeded by another straight-bladed pattern in 1796 (with shell-guards in addition to the knucklebow of the previous one), with sabres carried by grenadiers and light infantry, latterly of the 1803 pattern. This appears not to have been very popular; Kincaid referred to it as the 'small regulation half-moon sabre, better calculated to shave a lady's maid than a Frenchman's head',[95] and recalled how in one hand-to-hand fight an officer of the 95th Rifles made a blow with it which snapped off the blade, so smashed his opponent in the face with the hilt and finished him off with a kick. The broadsword with traditional basket hilt, carried by Highland regiments, was probably more useful on the rare occasions when such weapons were used in combat.

Similar distinctions applied in most other armies; for example, French officers carried a straight-bladed *épée*, but in *élite* companies, a sabre. In

Below: Hungarian grenadiers rush into action at the battle of Neresheim (11 August 1796), the man in the foreground firing as he advances. (Print after Wolff.)

Right: Austrian infantry sabres for grenadiers (with knuckle-bow) and for fusiliers. For Prima Plana (senior NCO) ranks the grenadier sabre was produced with gilded fittings (other ranks brass), and sometimes with lion-head pommel; the 1809 grenadier sabre had iron fittings. The curved brass quillons on the fusilier sabre were introduced in 1784, replacing the earlier straight quillons.

Far right:Sabres were universally popular for officers of élite or 'flank' companies (grenadiers and light infantry), but not infrequently were considerably different in design from established regulation patterns, as in the case of this British example with brass hilt and bone grip.

Right: British officers' swords. Top: 1803 flank company sabre. Bottom: left, 1803 flank company sabre; centre, 1786-style 'spadroon' with straight blade, the locket around the grip often bearing regimental identification; right, 1796-pattern battalion company sword, with straight blade and with one of the guards hinged to fold flat.

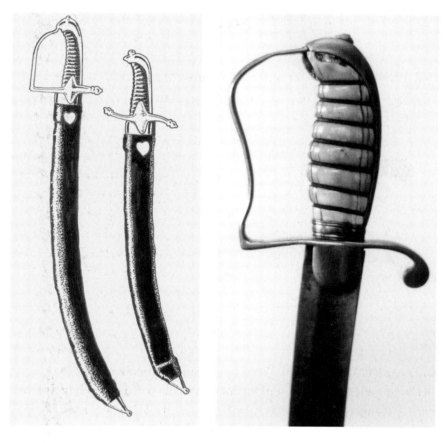

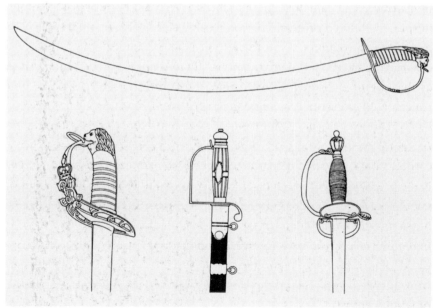

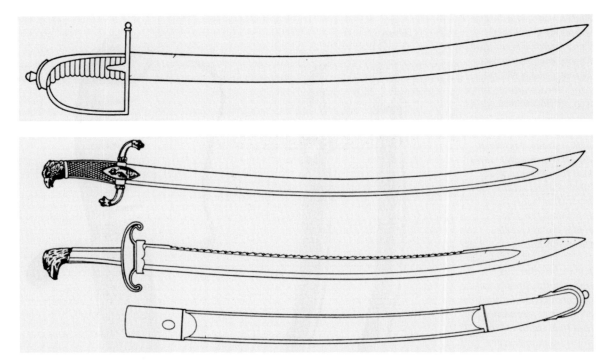

the Austrian Army, only in 1798 was an attempt made to standardise the design of officers' swords, and in addition to the usual distinctions, all officers of Hungarian regiments carried a sabre, that being regarded as a particular national weapon. Many officers in all armies preferred non-regulation weapons – 'Mameluke'-hilted sabres were quite popular, for example, despite the limited protection given to the hand by this oriental style, with quillons set at right-angles to the grip instead of a knucklebow. Some officers carried older, 'heirloom' weapons, but perhaps none so distinguished as that used by Colonel John Downie, the commander of a Spanish unit (uncharitably described as consisting of 'absurd, theatrically-dressed varlets'!)[96] known as the Estremaduran Legion or the *Cuerpo Volante de Leales de Pizarro*, who wore a mock sixteenth-century costume. Downie carried a long, gold-inlaid Spanish rapier which had previously belonged to Francisco Pizarro and which had been presented to him by a descendant of the conquistador. At the attack on Seville in August 1812 Downie leaped his horse into the French defences, but finding that his men had not followed him, threw the sword back towards them before he was wounded and captured. The rapier was recovered by an artillery officer and restored to Downie when the injured man was abandoned at the wayside by the retreating French.

Top: A precursor of the familiar sabre-briquet: a French grenadier sabre, 1790, with brass hilt.

Below: Representatives of the very decorative and singular patterns of sword carried by certain specialist troops. Top, French drum-major's sabre; bottom, French pioneer's sabre with serrated edge.

Right: The spadroon: a handsome design of sword as carried by British infantry officers 1786–96, but which had a somewhat fragile knuckle-bow. This example bears the crest of the East India Company upon the grip-locket.

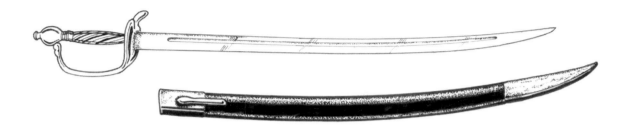

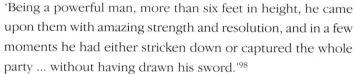

Above: Russian infantry sabre; brass fittings, the grip with diagonal grooving and the blade with a narrow fuller.

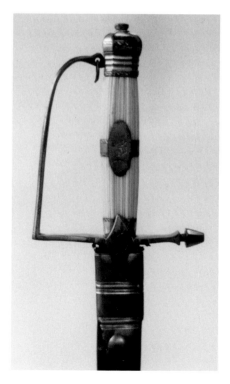

Some officers clearly had little confidence in the sword as a weapon: writing of the 1796 infantry pattern, which he thought good for neither cut nor thrust, Cavalié Mercer commented: 'Nothing could be more useless or more ridiculous ... a perfect encumbrance. In the foot artillery ... we generally wore dirks instead.'[97] Some carried other weapons in combat: for example, it was remarked that the unusual feat of Captain George Dansey of the British 88th at Busaco, where he was said to have killed three Frenchmen, was possible because he carried a musket, and a similar incident related to the captain of the 50th's grenadiers at Corunna. He habitually carried a heavy blackthorn stick, and jumped in among six French sharpshooters:

'Being a powerful man, more than six feet in height, he came upon them with amazing strength and resolution, and in a few moments he had either stricken down or captured the whole party ... without having drawn his sword.'[98]

The short swords carried by the rank-and-file of some armies were probably of very little practical use, as perhaps suggested if the French term for such a weapon, *sabre briquet*, were derived from the verb *bricoler*, to potter about or rake a fire. While it was sensible for NCOs and musicians to carry a sword, if they had no other weapon, for others it was probably more symbolic than of practical use. Most infantry swords were short and slightly curved, though they could be straight-bladed like the *Faschinenmesser* carried by Prussian Fusiliers, with a single-bar hilt. The French, for example, originally used the 1767-pattern sabre, replaced by those of *An IX* and *An XI*, which had a slightly more curved blade and a curved knucklebow, with a ribbed grip cast in one piece. (The ribbing was intended to facilitate handling, but was most effective when not deeply grooved: as was remarked about the later Brunswick rifle bayonet, more obvious grooves cut the bare palm worse than a schoolmaster's cane.) There also existed separate patterns carried by the Imperial Guard, but in the line regiments the issue of swords was generally restricted to NCOs, musicians and *élite* companies (an order of 1807 which withdrew them from *voltigeurs* seems not to have been obeyed universally). Austrian grenadiers carried a short sabre with curved knucklebow, but fusiliers originally had the 1784 sabre, shorter than the grenadier pattern (53cm against 67cm; 21in against 26.5in) and with no knucklebow, only quillons, but except for grenadiers, NCOs and musicians the sabre was withdrawn in 1798. The Prussian infantry sabre had small shell-guards as well as a knucklebow, until in 1818 a copy of the French *sabre-briquet* was authorised; Russian infantry swords followed the same design, a *briquet*-style version being introduced in 1817.

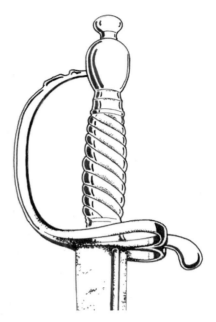

Some of the bayonets carried by rifle-armed troops could double as a sword, having hand-grips (for example like that of the Austrian 1779 *Jäger* rifle), conceivably derived from hunting-swords, and even a stirrup-hilt or knucklebow (like the first and second patterns respectively for the British Baker

Above: Prussian infantry sabre: brass hilt, short, slightly curved blade 59cm (23.2in) long. This style of hilt, with both knuckle-bow and small shell-guards, remained in use into the nineteenth century.

Left: French sabre-briquet of the classic design, later copied by a number of armies; with scabbard and bayonet-scabbard, and shoulder-belt with combined frog for both scabbards. The sabre has a woollen 'washer' at the base of the blade to prevent moisture entering the scabbard.

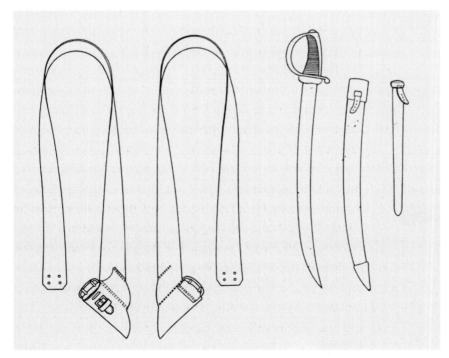

Above: Austrian fusiliers in the uniform of 1798; the man at the right is ramming a charge down his musket with great care to avoid impaling himself on his fixed bayonet. (Print after R. von Ottenfeld.)

rifle. From this came the continuing use of the term 'sword' instead of 'bayonet' in the Rifle Brigade, extending even to the command 'Fix Swords!').

The practical utility of the infantry sword might be suggested by Frederick the Great's punishment of his Bernburg Regiment after it had been defeated at Dresden in 1760: officers and NCOs were ordered to remove the lace from their hats, and the men to give up their swords. Given that the army was in the middle of a campaign, it would not seem to be a sensible punishment – had depriving them of their swords been considered as reducing the unit's future effectiveness in combat.

POLEARMS AND ARCHERY

Although the pike had become redundant by the early eighteenth century, it was an easily constructed weapon and thus saw some use in the Napoleonic era as a means of arming troops for whom no muskets were available. Thousands of 8- and 10-foot (2.4 and 3 metre) pikes were produced by France during the emergency of 1792–3, and at similar times elsewhere, though generally replaced by firearms at the first opportunity. For example, they were carried by a few British volunteer corps, Russian *opolchenie* (militia) in 1812, and in the guise of sharpened vine-poles, by Portuguese *ordenança*, and as late as March 1814 it was reported that the National Guard of Paris had begun 'to use the newly fabricated lances'.[99] Agricultural implements, or weapons derived from them, were also pushed into use, for example the scythes of the Polish patriot forces in 1794 and by the Vendéean rebels. (A notable exhortation to use such weapons was issued by the governor of Moscow, Feodor Rostopchin, in 1812, calling on

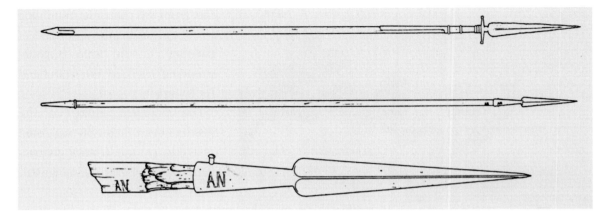

the civilian population to take up arms against the invaders, 'particularly pitchforks, which are so much more suitable against the French, because in weight they resemble trusses of straw'![100])

In addition to weapons issued in emergency, some commentators actually advocated the reintroduction of pikes as a protection for musketeers instead of bayonets. Even twenty years after the end of the Napoleonic Wars, John Mitchell was advocating three-deep phalanxes of pikemen, equipped with shields, to rush upon the enemy and decide battles hand-to-hand, which he thought was a more humane form of warfare than costly musketry-duels, and in support of his theory cited earlier authorities including the Prussians Georg Heinrich von Berenhorst and Dietrich von Bülow, Maurice de Saxe and the Chevalier de Folard (of whom the last two had died some nineteen and seventeen years respectively before Napoleon was born!) Others recommended pikes for particular duties, such as the storm of defended positions. A story quoted in support of this theory involved Suvarov, who was said to have ordered his lancers and cossacks to cut their lances in half to produce a short, pike-like weapon before such a storm, remarking that if they were killed, the loss of the lances would not matter, and if they were victorious, new lances could be procured! Indeed, pikes could be effective in the hands of determined men, and against troops of mediocre quality, but were of limited use in close combat. A large proportion of the Irish insurgent forces in 1798 were armed only with pikes, and the battle of New Ross was quoted to demonstrate the weapon's weakness: the insurgents' courage initially drove back their enemies, but when the latter returned to the attack and fighting took place in the streets, under such circumstances the pikes were found to be unmanageable, and high casualties were incurred in unequal combat against muskets and bayonets.

Above: Polearms: top: British sergeants' spontoon, with cross-bar below the head to prevent over-penetration; bottom, French An IV pike with detail of a typical blade.

Right: The archaic polearm still in use: an officer of Russian Foot Guards carrying a half-pike, 1801. (Print after Jacquemin.)

In conjunction with musketeers the pike might have been of more use. A deliberate experiment was made in the US Army in 1812–13, by the appropriately named explorer, Colonel Zebulon Pike. In his 15th Infantry Regiment he had the first two ranks armed in the conventional manner with muskets and bayonets, but the third rank carried ash pikes 10 or 11 feet long (3–3.3 metres), so that in combat they would reach over the front ranks to give the effect of a third rank of bayonets. The pikemen were armed with shortened muskets, about 18 inches (46 cm) having been taken off the barrels, which they slung on their backs, and with swords to compensate the loss of their bayonets. The regiment was armed thus in the operations against York in April 1813, but after Pike's death in the explosion of the magazine there the experiment was abandoned.[101] (It is interesting to note that a British writer had proposed exactly the same scheme in 1799.[102])

At times during the Napoleonic Wars pikes were used, sometimes with considerable effect, by naval landing-parties, equipped with short boarding-pikes. Under certain circumstances they may even have been more effective than muskets; in the attack on Banda Neira in 1810, for example, an assault by British naval pikemen captured a battery of ten guns 'without a musket being fired'[103] and thus without alerting the remainder of the enemy garrison. At Acre in 1799 a sally was mounted against the French siege-works by British seamen armed with pikes, a 'desperate service'[104] which succeeded in interrupting the construction of a mine, though it is perhaps significant that the phalanx of pikemen was protected on each flank by a spirited attack by Ottoman troops, who carried back from the sally some sixty severed enemy heads 'as proof of their prowess'!

In addition to pikes, polearms were used in a number of armies (for example Prussia and Russia) as marks of commissioned or NCO rank, but upon the modernisation of these armies such things were dis-

carded. (The partisans carried by Russian officers caused some surprise to British witnesses
who saw them in the Netherlands in 1799,
notably from the fact that when they passed a
general in review, they twirled them around
their heads like a drum-major.) British 'battalion company' officers carried spontoons (or
espontoons: half-pikes) until 1786, and from
1792 the sergeants' halberds were replaced by
spontoons, which were retained until 1830.
(Unlike conventional pikes, they had a cross-bar
below the head to prevent over-penetration.)
They were not popular, as exemplified by a
British sergeant who recalled how, due to casualties among the officers, he had to carry the
battalion Colours at Salamanca, 'a circumstance
which served as a good pretext for throwing
away my pike: a useless piece of military furniture'.[105] They could even be dangerous to the
bearer: John Cooper recalled how in the
Peninsula a sergeant of the Foot Guards had an
accident while chasing a pig, when 'the point of
his pike ran into the earth and stuck fast, causing the butt-end to pass through his body',[106]
but he recovered.

As one commentator observed: 'Posterity
will hardly believe, that four centuries after the
invention of gunpowder, the non-commissioned officers in the British army were still
armed with pikes ... the most intelligent and the
most expert in the use of arms, left totally without the means of defence.'[107] Nevertheless,
these weapons were used in combat: a witness
of Busaco, for example, remembered how
Sergeant Pat Brazil of the British 88th 'killed a
Frenchman, by the push of his halbert, who had
nearly overpowered his Captain'[108] and at
Waterloo Sergeant Christopher Switzer of the

32nd ran-through a French officer who had tried to seize the regiment's Colour. Another use of the spontoon was recorded at Waterloo, to preserve order in the ranks, as a sergeant of the 3/1st Foot Guards recalled: 'The fight, at one time, was so desperate with our battalion, that files upon files were carried out to the rear from the carnage, and the line was held up by the sergeants' pikes placed against the rear – not for want of courage on the men's parts (for they were desperate), only for the moment our loss so unsteadied the line.'[109]

Other polearms were carried by certain selected personnel: from 1808, for example, *deuxième* and *troisième porte-aigles* in the French infantry (NCOs who guarded the officer who carried the 'Eagle' Colour) were usually equipped with halberds, and a regimental tradition led to grenadier sergeants of the French 102nd Line carrying a military version of a medieval 'military fork', a weapon derived originally from an agricultural pitchfork but which became a proper military polearm in medieval warfare.

In 1776 Benjamin Franklin suggested to General Charles Lee that given the imperfections in the musket, pikes and bows and arrows might be considered as a substitute, as a competent archer would certainly be able to fire more quickly than a musketeer. The only archery recorded in the Napoleonic Wars seems to have been that practised by some of Russia's Asiatic irregular light cavalry, but perhaps rather strangely, it was not entirely discounted. The increase of archery as a gentlemanly sport in the later eighteenth century probably led to the occasional thought about its military use: in Britain in 1784, for example, the uniformed Toxopholite Society became associated to the Honourable Artillery Company, of which it formed a flank division, and members agreed to wear bayonets on duty. In 1792 a meeting of the Societies of Archers at Blackheath was attended not only by the HAC and such clubs as the Surrey Bowmen and the Woodmen of Arden, but most of the prizes were gained by the Royal Artillery Archers. Inevitably one theorist, Richard O. Mason, published a plan for the arming of a corps of archers with bows for offence and pikes for protection,[110] and even provided an appropriate drill, but despite all the advantages set forth by its supporters (including a claim that an experienced bowman could shoot twelve shafts per minute), the bow never returned to use, if for no other reason that it took years of practice to produce the sort of proficient archer who had proved such a force in the Hundred Years War.

An example of the impracticality of some military theorists is exemplified by this imaginary uniform designed for a corps of British archers, armed with bows and pikes, from Mason's treatise on the reintroduction of the British longbow.

The ideal of manoeuvre in precise formation must frequently have been impossible to attain in the field: British infantry advance at Toulouse. (Print after H. Dupray.)

INFANTRY SERVICE

SKIRMISHING

Although the infantry tactics of the period were characterised to a considerable extent by manoeuvre in large and closely packed formations, one of the most significant features of the French Revolutionary Wars was the development and expansion of light infantry tactics. Earlier in the eighteenth century light infantry had been used as an adjunct to the usual combat formations of column and line, and their tactics had been practised to some effect in the Seven Years War and in North America, but in many cases had retrogressed with lack of use since those campaigns. Much of the earlier light troop function had been provided not by line troops, but irregulars most suited to light infantry service, like the expert Austro-Hungarian *Grenzers* (border troops) and various *Jäger* corps, whose slow-loading rifles made then unsuited to act in line. Some such corps did exist during the Napoleonic era, but one key to the development of light infantry service was the flexibility of line troops to act as light infantry: Sir John Moore exemplified the essentials of this flexibility when instructing his battalion of militia light companies in Ireland in 1798–9: 'Our Light Infantry ... are in fact a mixture of the Yager [sic], and the Grenadier'.[111]

From the early stages of the French Revolutionary Wars it became customary for French infantry attacks (generally mounted in column) to be preceded by a host of skirmishers, sometimes deployed so thickly that they could be mistaken for an advancing, formed line. Although in the French Army (as in most others) some elements might be trained specifically for skirmish duties, all were capable of performing this service, so that not just specialist companies but whole battalions, even whole brigades, might be thrown forward as skirmishers. General Philibert Duhesme remarked that by the end of 1793 the French had *only* light infantry, and it became an established tactic to deploy as much as one-fifth of a division *en débandade* (in open order: lit. 'in confusion') as *tirailleurs* (sharpshooters), holding back the remainder either to reinforce the skirmish-screen or to deliver a full attack when the skirmish-fire had sufficiently weakened the enemy. The ability of all French troops to perform these duties proficiently gave them a huge advantage over their less flexible opponents.

There were several advantages in engaging the enemy with a skirmish-line. Skirmishers in 'open order', sometimes taking advantage of natural cover, would not present so massed a target as a line, and thus would suffer fewer casualties from artillery or musketry; and by firing not to order but at will, and often deliberately aimed, would gall and disorder the enemy line whose situation would be worsened by its comparatively ineffectual reply. Skirmishers would also often screen from enemy view the manoeuvres of their supports or of the main attack

Above: Skirmishing: French infantry are attacked by Austrian heavy cavalry, c. 1796. (Engraving after Horace Vernet.)

which they were preceding. Unless the enemy had skirmishers of equal proficiency, a skirmish-line would generally have the advantage. As a Spanish commentator noted, volley-firing not only reduced the efficiency of a line's musketry (by fouling of barrels and chipping of flints), but the comparative ineffectiveness of it would cause the defenders to lose confidence. Troops in line unable to make a decisive advance (skirmishers might only fall back before them and continue their sharpshooting) might be devastated by skirmish-fire. Albeit something of an exceptional case, in that they were allowed to remain under such fire much longer than necessary, the ordeal of the gallant Prussian infantry at Vierzehnheiligen during the Battle of Jena demonstrates what skirmish-fire could achieve. Against French sharpshooters under cover, they tried to reply by volley-firing but for two hours were shot down in droves; Maude described it as 'one of the most extraordinary and pitiful incidents in military history'.[112]

Light infantry service demanded not only adequate training, but a level of initiative and independence much greater than that required of a 'line' soldier; as was remarked of the more modern weapons, 'The old musket was the arm of the masses, and the rifle is that of the individual.'[113] Some of the requisite aspects of light infantry service were not easy for the more reactionary parts of the military establishment to accept, and were even

Above: The confusion of the skirmish-line is suggested by this study of French infantry, c. 1805. (Engraving after Horace Vernet.)

Right: French troops in Egypt improvising a firing-line to protect savants (scholars examining the antiquities of the country) from Mameluke attack. On a number of occasions, as here, the scientists had to assist in repelling attacks. (Engraving after Horace Vernet.)

satirised: 'Mr Grimaldi, of Covent-Garden Theatre, has been recommended, we understand, to the new corps of *Yagers* [*sic*], about to be raised, as their posture-master; having displayed so much ingenious agility in walking upon his head, standing upon his shoulders, crawling upon his belly, running on his back, and hopping on his knees'![114] To Sir John Moore, who with his associates was one of the principal developers of light infantry tactics in the British Army, the requisite development of independence and initiative required a new form of discipline, what he termed the discipline of mind as well as of body. Moore's assistant, Lieutenant-Colonel Kenneth Mackenzie, [115] described the essence of this: 'The only way of having a regiment in good order was by every individual thoroughly knowing and performing his duty ... the best and surest method was to commence drilling the whole of the officers, and when they became perfectly acquainted with the system, they could teach the men, and by their zeal, knowledge, and above all, good temper and kind treatment of the soldier, make the regiment the best in the service.'[116] The result, as George Napier stated, was to lead officers 'to look upon the soldier as a

fellow-citizen, who, by the admitted laws of society and for the general good of the State placed under you in rank and station, is nevertheless as good a man and as good a Christian as yourself, born in the same country, amenable to the same laws, and above all possessing the same feelings as the proudest peer in the land'.[117] Such concepts were so alien to the attitudes of the more reactionary elements of military establishments that it is not surprising if in some cases it inhibited the development of light infantry tactics.

The essence of successful skirmish tactics was described by a manual of 1803:

> Vigilance, activity, and intelligence, are particularly requisite ... Rapidity of movement is one of the chief characteristics of light infantry. It is this which establishes their own security, at the same time that it renders them the terror of the enemy ... The intelligence chiefly required in a light infantry man is, that he should know how to take advantage of every circumstance of ground which can enable him to harass and annoy an enemy, without exposing himself ... Light infantry must know how to gain upon an enemy along hedges, through corn fields, amongst gardens and ditches, almost without

Left: Riflemen firing from cover: characteristic tactics depicted in this illustration of Charles Random de Berenger, adjutant of the Duke of Cumberland's Sharpshooters (and a perpetrator of the Stock Exchange fraud of 1814!); note the riflemen taking advantage of natural cover, and the whistle worn around Berenger's neck, a common method of transmitting orders. (Aquatint by Reinagle after Berenger.)

Right: *Skirmishing: Grenadiers à Pied of Napoleon's Imperial Guard drive off enemy cavalry. (Print after Horace Vernet.)*

Right: *Skirmishing: Grenadiers à Pied of Napoleon's Imperial Guard drive off enemy cavalry. (Print after Horace Vernet.)*

being perceived ... Against regular infantry formed ... in close order ... they must hover round these continually in every quarter. If the regulars advance rapidly upon them, the light troops must recede; and when the enemy is exhausted ... they must again line the hedges and ditches round him on every side. In such a situation light infantry can be opposed not otherwise than by men acting in the same manner with themselves ... light troops should all be expert marksmen. *To fire seldom and always with effect* should be their chief study ... Noise and smoke is not sufficient to stop the advance of soldiers accustomed to war; they are to be checked only by seeing their comrades fall.[118]

Or, as George Hanger remarked, 'though the enemy fired at be not wounded, yet the ball passes so close to him as to intimidate, and prove to him how skilful an opponent he is engaged with ... when a corps of ... good marksmen engage an enemy ... and never pull a trigger without deliberate and positive good aim, provided that they are not fortunate enough to kill, they are sure to intimidate'.[119]

Skirmish-lines were sometimes so dense that they were mistaken for a formed line (for example, French accounts make it clear that they mistook the British skirmishers at Barrosa for a first line of formed troops). In British service, for example, in regulation 'open order' the files were only two feet (61cm) apart, in 'extended order' two paces. Certain tactics were recommended fairly generally, for example that skirmishers should fire from the right of any cover, to reveal themselves as little as possible, and that they should advance or retire obliquely to present the most difficult (moving) target.

Left: An uncomfortable but effective mode of rifle-shooting, lying on the back and bracing the rifle with the sling around the leg: Thomas Plunket of the British 95th shoots General Auguste de Colbert at Cacabellos. (Print after Harry Payne.)

Skirmishers might be deployed in two lines, one moving through the gaps in the other, in either advance or retreat; or could operate in pairs, one covering the other, as described by a British manual: 'As soon as the front rank man has fired, he is to slip to the left of the rear man, who will make a short pace forward, and put himself in the other's place, whom he is to protect while loading. When the first man returns his ramrod, he will give his comrade the word *ready*, after which, and not before, he may fire, and immediately change places as before.'[120] The hazards of not having a 'comrade' to provide cover are exemplified in a story concerning a single Portuguese skirmisher who engaged a single Frenchman. After an exchange of shots, the Portuguese fell as if dead, whereupon the Frenchman, without waiting to reload, ran forward to plunder the body before anyone else could reach it; and was thus helpless when, as he drew near, the unharmed Portuguese jumped up and shot him dead.

It was held generally that skirmishers should never be left unsupported. When one or more companies of a line battalion were thrown forward to skirmish, the main body might act as a reserve, or a proportion of the skirmishers could be held back, to be fed into the skirmish-line, or to cover its retreat, as necessary. This might considerably reduce the volume of fire which a unit could deliver. According to the Austrian regulations of 1807, for example, one-third of the skirmishers were deployed, one-third formed an immediate support 100 paces back, and the remaining third provided a reserve a further 100 paces to the rear. Under the Saxon system, only one-quarter of their *Jägers* should actually have deployed, with a quarter formed in line some distance to the rear, and the remaining half forming a second reserve yet farther back. Some questions were raised about the best method of reinforcing a skirmish-line: for example, Denis Davidov said that troops fed in from the rear might impede the skirmish-line, whereas the system adopted by General Kulnev in Finland in 1808, of positioning the supports on the flanks, enabled flank-attacks to be made upon the enemy if the original skirmish-force had to fall back.[121] If skirmishers had to fall back upon an advancing main body, to clear the ground for the latter, an effective tactic was to gather the skirmishers into one or more small groups and fall back on the flanks of, or through the intervals in, the advancing formed bodies, and reassemble at their rear.

The fact the some troops – especially those armed with rifles – were best suited exclusively to skirmish duties, led to varied systems of deployment. Marmont, for example, advocated the forming of two distinct types of light troops. Remarking that some light infantry regiments – notably those of France and Russia – were little different from the line, he recommended that regimental light companies (e.g., *voltigeurs*) be used to supply their immediate needs, but that each larger formation should have strong battalions of *bona fide* light infantry attached, suited specifically for skirmish duties (like the Austrian *Jägers*). This, in fact, was similar to the manner in which rifle companies were deployed by the British in the Peninsula, whereby each division had extra light troops attached in addition to those of each component battalion. (One member of the Light Division, in fact, remarked that it would have been preferable had the parts of this formation been deployed similarly, rather than concentrating a large proportion of the army's most expert light troops into the one division.) The same commentator lamented the fact that some line battalions left all skirmishing to their light company, giving the remainder no training in skirmish tactics. Even the deployment of such regimental light companies might vary, if those of several units were concentrated into specialist battalions, much in the way that the Austrian grenadiers, for example, were habitually detached from their regiments. Such organisations, however, were sometimes far from permanent, but might be formed for a specific task. Probably the loosest of all such arrangements was that adopted by the British in the Peninsula and Waterloo campaigns, in which the battalion light companies of a brigade were ordered to 'act together as a battalion of light infantry, under the command of a Field Officer or Captain, to be selected for the occasion by the General Officer commanding the brigade, upon all occasions on which the brigade may be formed in line or column, whether for a march or to oppose the enemy',[122] but on *all* other occasions the light companies were to remain part of their battalions.

Light infantry training might be extended beyond those troops so designated. Under the Archduke Charles's reforms, for example, the third rank of Austrian line regiments could be withdrawn to form *ad hoc* platoons for use either as an advance-guard or reserve, or to act as skirmishers. This was by no means a new process: a similar expedient had been adopted in the Prussian Army as early as 1787, when ten men from each infantry company were trained as light infantry, armed with rifles and designated *Schützen* (sharpshooters), to supplement the fusilier battalions created at the same time, but the system was abolished after Jena. (Evidently it had not worked as well as intended: instead of providing each battalion with its own light infantry section, in many cases the *Schützen* were detached from their parent corps to form composite units, the reverse of the original intention.) According to the Prussian 1812 regulations, although all fusiliers were trained as skirmishers, they were intended to be deployed as such only when circumstances dictated; when acting in line alongside the ordinary musketeer battalions, they used only their third rank as skirmishers, like the remainder.

Failure to concentrate a battalion's skirmishers into a particular company was criticised by some commentators; one remarked that by training some men of each company as light infantry 'you may lose ... the services of both; because the active may be of no use, being kept back by their sluggish companions; and unless they are previously divided into separate bodies, you cannot distinguish and separate them when wanted'[123] (although this could be avoided by selecting men specifically according to their abilities). Some units appear to have trained extra men in addition to those designated as light infantry: the practice was sanctioned officially for the British in the Mediterranean, for example, which allowed men designated as 'flankers' to be concentrated into a light battalion at Maida. In some cases this practice may have continued: at Quatre Bras, for example, the collected light companies of Kempt's Brigade were described as being augmented by one whole company of the 79th, and by the 'marksmen' of that regiment. There are also plenty of instances of non-specialist companies, or even entire line battalions, being deployed in open order where the situation required: for example, when at Busaco Alexander Wallace of the British 88th observed the French light troops overpowering those in his front, he ordered out a file from each of his companies to reinforce the skirmish-screen. Such men might not have been as expert as those specially trained for light infantry duties, but many seem to have managed well enough, even though the system was not always successful. For example, Edward Macready of the British 30th, recalled how, while his light company had been absent at the beginning of the Battle of Quatre Bras, one of the other companies had 'endeavoured to skirmish'[124] and had suffered heavily. Troops who were very inexpert at skirmishing might be at a fatal disadvantage: a notable example was quoted from Egypt in 1807 when three British companies were surrounded by wretchedly armed Albanian sharpshooters; perhaps because they were not sufficiently trained to reply in kind, they formed square, the worst possible formation for presenting an easy target, and were forced to surrender.

The contemporary belief that certain characteristics could be ascribed to different nationalities was evident in the assessment of light infantry; for example, one writer asserted that Hungarians were the most ideally suited of any, from natural resourcefulness, hardihood and an outdoor existence in their civilian life. A great deal, however, depended upon training and practical experience in the field. At Vimeiro, for instance, the British 43rd (later one of the best light corps in the army) were entirely outmatched by the more experienced French skirmishers. So much more were the companies of 'battalion' men to reinforce the hard-pressed light infantry: 'Getting bewildered among the corn-fields and olives, the young hands scarce knew which way to turn, the old ones, too, were puzzled, and when a blaze of musketry opened on them, from they knew not where, they were literally mowed down, falling like ninepins among the standing corn; the remnant was soon flung back ... leaving the scene of the action mottled by their slain.'[125] Only the few riflemen, properly trained in taking cover, were able to meet the French on even terms.

Some armies were known quite widely for their inability to match the skirmishing proficiency of the French. Austria's *Grenzers* seem to have become more like line infantry, and their 'line' skirmishers, even after the reforms of the Archduke Charles, were still controlled rigidly and received little training in independent movement. Skirmishing tended to be regarded as basically a defensive counter to the enemy's skirmishers, and even Austrian officers admitted that the army did not fully understand the entire idea of skirmishing. Similarly, even after the experience of the Napoleonic Wars, it was remarked how rigidly the Russian Army deployed its skirmish-

ers, as if in an extension of the perfection of their column and line manoeuvres, not taking advantage of terrain features and instead of looking about
them to spot available cover, all eyes were kept fixed upon their officers.

Even in armies that did have some proficiency, there might be much ignorance of what was actually required. An example was quoted concerning a
lieutenant of the British 34th at Toulouse who, while under heavy fire,
observed three riflemen of the 60th taking cover behind a stone wall. He
called to them to stand up boldly and not hide, whereupon two were killed
immediately, a senseless loss caused by an officer not understanding his
duties. A similarly futile waste was observed by Sir Thomas Graham at
Borghetto in 1796, when an Austrian regiment lost some 150 men to French
skirmish-fire when a withdrawal of only six yards would have sheltered
them, had their pride and bravery allowed it. Presumed ignorance of skir-
mish-tactics might even cause a unit to withdraw in the face of its own retiring skirmishers who had been mistaken for the enemy; such an incident was
actually recorded at Jena. When troops were outmatched in skirmishing

ability they might resort to other measures: an
example was described by Captain William
Burney of the British 44th at Quatre Bras. His battalion was confronted by French skirmishers firing from rye so high that it concealed them
entirely, and as the 44th's own skirmishers were
unable to match them, they were called in by
their commander and a more old-fashioned tactic
was employed: file-firing from the main body,
hoping to drive off the invisible enemy by sweep-
ing the rye with volleys of musketry.[126]

Although skirmish-order might not be ideal
for full attacks, it could be used as more than just
the prelude to such an attack. Massed attacks by
skirmishers proved effective for the French on
many occasions, so that in some cases the sup-
porting troops themselves dispersed into skirmish-order to mount an attack. An example
occurred at Jena when elements of Desjardin's
division advanced behind their skirmishers and
then lost their formation, instead rushing on successfully in open order.

THE LINE

Skirmishing apart, the concept of the Napoleonic Wars being contested by large blocks of men, with battalions forming the basic manoeuvre element, is true only in part. Fairly rigid formations did form the cornerstone of battlefield manoeuvre, for which the integrity of tactical formations – brigades, divisions and *corps d'armées* – was an essential ingredient in the transmission of orders and in co-ordinated manoeuvres. This was not, however, a universal rule: sub-units might be deployed individually if circumstances demanded, companies might be fed into a fight in small numbers, whole battalions might be deployed as skirmishers, and units might be detached from their parent formations for specific tasks. These expedients occurred even in armies with as sophisticated an organisation as had Napoleon's, with commanders using their resources irrespective of their official brigade or divisional allocation. Such flexibility could prove to be of considerable consequence on the battlefield.

The three basic formations used in actions were columns (for virtually all movement), lines (for maximum firepower), and squares (as a defence against cavalry). Within each of these formations there were numerous variations, and a vital necessity was the ability to change from one formation to another as rapidly as possible. Certain basic evolutions had to become almost automatic if a unit were to be able to operate proficiently, and indeed this was necessary for their own security; but some of the manoeuvres practised on the parade ground were probably of very little use on the field of battle.

A similar case was the speed of march: using the official manoeuvre-regulations, calculations might be made regarding the comparative rapidity with which units could move, change formation or deploy. In the context of the battlefield, such calculations could be significant in determining, for example, how many volleys a battalion might have to face when making an advance; but contemporary experiments, like that of William Duane, who

Left: On the march: a voltigeur (left) and carabinier of French light infantry, 1809. (Print after Hippolyte Bellangé.)

Right: company in three ranks, from the French 1791 regulations, showing the positioning of officers and NCOs.
  C: Captain
  L: Lieutenant
  S: Sergeant
  SL: Sous-lieutenant (junior lieutenant)
  SM: sergeant-major

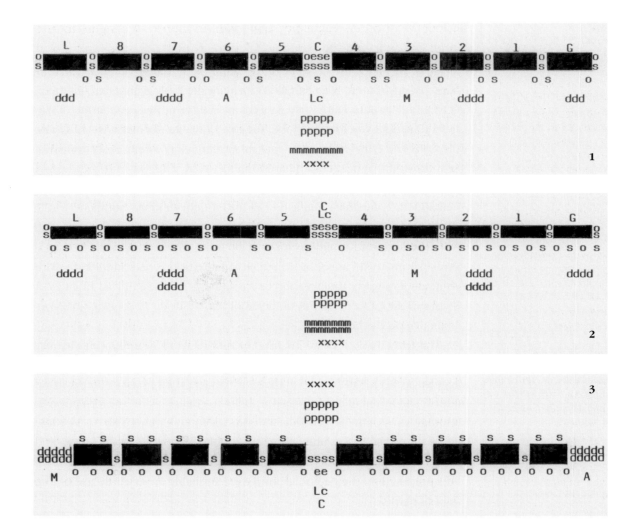

found that a company in line advanced 250 yards (229 metres) in two minutes twenty-five seconds (including a 'charge' at the end) were conducted
mostly under ideal conditions. In the same way that calculations based upon
the speed of march decreed in manoeuvre-regulations might be applicable
only on the parade-ground, such statistics might not have much relevance
to manoeuvres conducted over broken terrain, amid the smoke and stress
of battle and with formations disrupted by the fall of casualties to enemy
fire. The reality seems to have been recognised by an essay of 1800 which
implied that no greater precision could be attained than the statement that
'infantry can advance 100, nay 120 paces in a minute, without running'.[127]

A crucial point was made by Dundas's British Regulations: that 'movements are intended to be made with the greatest quickness, that is con-

Left:

1 *and* **2** *It is likely that not even contemporary drill-manuals are an infallible guide to what actually occurred. These diagrams show a British infantry battalion in line in close order, showing the position of officers, NCOs and others. The first, from the 1798 edition of Dundas's official manual, shows significant variations from the second, Dickinson's elucidation of the latter, published in the same year, and based upon the version of the drill employed by the Coldstream Guards.*

Key: companies numbered 1–8, plus G (grenadiers) and L (light company), shown as solid black.
A: *adjutant*
C: *colonel*
d: *drummer*
e: *ensign with Colour*
Lc: *lieutenant-colonel*
M: *major*
m: *musician*
o: *officer*
p: *pioneer*
s: *sergeant*
x: *staff officer*

3 *A variation on the battalion drawn up in line: a battalion assembled in open order. Key as above.*

sistent with order, regularity, and without hurry or fatigue to the troops'.[128] Such was the importance of preservation of order over speed that Dundas reduced his pace from the first edition of his work to that which was adopted officially (quick time, for example, reducing from 120 to 108 paces per minute).

Most armies had at least two rates of march, some considerably more; the British, for example, had an 'ordinary time' of 75 paces to the minute, 'quick time' of 108 paces and 'wheeling step' for manoeuvring of 120 paces; with each pace of 30 inches (76cm), the distance thus covered per minute was 62.5, 90 and 100 yards (57, 82 and 91 metres) respectively. The French used a step of 65cm (25.6in), an ordinary step of 76 paces to the minute, quick step of 100 and manoeuvre pace of 120 (54, 71.1 and 85.3 yards ; 49.4, 65 and 78 metres per minute respectively). Similarly, at ordinary pace Austrian infantry marched at about 63 yards (58 metres) per minute, Prussian infantry at 52 yards (47.5 metres) per minute, which might suggest that the French ability to march was inferior to some and equal to others; whereas in fact the French outmarched everybody, at least over the longer distances. Indeed, the ability to make forced marches and then fight at the end was one of the characteristics of Napoleon's system of war, a product both of training and morale. Marshal Michel Ney remarked that one of the greatest difficulties was to accustom the soldier to the fatigue of marching, but that the sobriety and physical condition of the French soldier made him pre-eminent. He stated that not just rapidity of march, but also the ability to make a combination of marches, was crucial to the outcome of a campaign, and that it was of paramount importance that troops should be trained to make forced marches with the same full equipment that they would carry in wartime.

The extent of that equipment emphasises the resilience of the ordinary soldier. John Cooper described the standard British kit (with weight in pounds in parentheses) as comprising: musket and bayonet (14), cartridge-box and ammunition (6), belts and equipment (9), clothing (20¼), provisions (8), miscellaneous (1¾), making 59 pounds (26.7kg). (He added that 'the government should also have sent us new backbones to bear the extra weight'.[129]

A number of remarkable feats of marching are recorded, such as that of the British Light Brigade to Talavera, evidently 42 miles in 26 hours, and then an additional four or five miles beyond Talavera. Even more impressive was the march of the British 10th Foot from Kilkenny to Dublin in winter

Above: Tired Italian infantry of Pino's Division of the Grande Armée on the march in Russia, July 1812. (Print after Albrecht Adam.)

weather in February 1760, when it was said they covered more than 71 miles in 24 hours. Yet where it was possible for many units to make one forced march, the French could keep going: in a period of fourteen days in 1806 Davout's Corps marched 166 miles and fought the Battle of Auerstädt. Such a sustained effort could be crippling; writing of a 36-hour forced march to Austerlitz, Elzéar Blaze remarked that one-twentieth of the whole arrived together, and the remainder who could not sustain the pace trailed in hour after hour behind them. Jean-Roch Coignet recalled 'marching by platoons all day and all night, and at last holding on to each other to prevent falling', and even of falling asleep while marching; hence the saying 'The Emperor makes war not with our arms but with our legs!'[130]

The line had been the primary formation for combat, and despite the importance of the column in the warfare of the period, it remained the best way of utilising firepower. The organisation of the line, however, varied. A common deployment was to draw up a line three men deep (the fashion generally used by the French), in which it was possible (though somewhat difficult) for all three ranks to use their muskets simultaneously. The most convenient method was probably by the process styled 'locking', in which the front rank sank on to the right knee, the centre rank took a pace backwards with the right foot, and the third rank took a pace to the right. As early as 1727 Humphrey Bland had remarked that this allowed the rear-rank men to fire over the right shoulders of the centre rank, avoiding the latter having to stoop to allow the rear men to fire over their heads, an 'inconvenient and uneasy posture'.[131] This system was prescribed, for example, by the Prussian manual of 1788, which remained in use until after the 1806 campaign.

Alternatively, the third rank could be withdrawn for such purposes as skirmishing (as mentioned before); this change was made in the 1812 Prussian regulations, for example, where in contrast to the previous system, only the first two ranks were ordered to fire (both standing), while the third rank was to retire a couple of steps so as not to impede the firers. Another system, included for example in the 1791 French regulations, was for the third-rank men to assist those in the second rank with their loading, with all ranks remaining standing. This process generally began by the ranks firing together, after which the first rank continued to fire as quickly as possible. The centre-rank man then took a loaded musket from the third rank, fired, reloaded it himself and fired again before passing it backwards and receiving another loaded musket, so that 'the man of the centre rank fires always twice with the same firelock, before he returns it to the man in his rear, excepting the first time',[132] with all firing subsequent to the first volley being at will. The greatest difficulty with this was evidently the danger that such musketry could degenerate into haphazard fire which was difficult to stop, especially if the third-rank men also began to fire on their own account, instead of being content just to load for the men in front; so Ney recommended that fire should be restricted

Below: The ability of three ranks to fire together, albeit in a somewhat awkward manner, is demonstrated by this engraving from a contemporary drill manual. The troops involved are members of the British 3rd Foot Guards in the uniform dating from March 1790 (when lace edging was removed from their hats) and September 1796, when the hat-loops were removed.

to a prelude to a charge, with the third rank held back as a reserve. There was also a very real danger that men in the front rank would be shot accidentally by the men behind, especially if the troops involved were inexperienced. It was stated that as many as a quarter of casualties were wounded in this way, and faced with almost 3,000 young soldiers having wounds in their hands or forearms in 1813, Napoleon ordered some to be shot as a punishment for what was presumed to be self-mutilation to escape further service. Larrey investigated and proved them all innocent, victims either of inadequate training in the arms-drill, with men shot by those behind them, or of advancing with

the musket held up when the hands would be the first part of the body to be hit.

The advantages of the third rank were described by Dundas, who claimed that the two-deep line 'is calculated only for light troops in the attack and pursuit of a timid enemy, but not for making an impression upon an opposite regular line'. A two-deep line, he averred, 'would never be brought to make or to stand an attack with bayonets, nor could it have any prospect of resisting the charge of a determined cavalry. In no service is the fire and consistency of the third rank given up; it serves to fill up the vacancies made in the others in action, without it the battalion would soon be in a single rank'. He did, however, permit the two-deep rank to be practised for occasions 'where an extended and covered front is to be occupied, or where an irregular enemy, who deals only in fire, is to be opposed',[133] or to enable an under-strength battalion to exercise with a full frontage. This shows how manuals might not reflect actual practice: although the three-deep line continued to be advocated until Torrens's revised regulations of 1824, the two-deep line was used almost universally by the British throughout the Napoleonic Wars.

Remarking especially on British practice, Marmont supported the two-rank line, claiming that the difference in solidity between two and three was negligible, that firing with three ranks was impracticable, and that in any case in combat the three ranks very soon resolved themselves spontaneously into two. The idea that the third-rank men should load for those in front he disclaimed as entirely impracticable under battlefield conditions. Furthermore, others were concerned that the third-rank men could make no use of their bayonets, and indeed it was claimed that Russian troops had accidentally killed one another when the third rank charged with levelled bayonets. In 1768 the Marquis de Silva proposed the issue of muskets and bayonets of different lengths, the longest for the third-rank men so that their bayonets would be on a level with those at the front, and an Austrian writer recommended much the same by having socket-hilted sword-bayonets of different lengths.

The French 1791 regulations had, in fact, authorised two-deep lines for peacetime manoeuvres, so as to occupy the same frontage as when augmented in strength to a war footing, and finally Napoleon himself recommended the use of two-rank lines. In October 1813 he ordered that this was to be the formation used henceforward, remarking that not only was the third rank largely useless with both musket and bayonet, but that as the enemy was used to seeing the French in three ranks, by forming in two (and thus extending the front) they would imagine the French to be one-third stronger than they actually were. At St Helena Napoleon stated that the third rank should either be given greater consistency, or suppressed.

An example of how what actually occurred could diverge from written practice was demonstrated at Waterloo, when towards the end of the day British battalions were assembled four-deep, ostensibly for extra solidity. This was criticised as 'a sacrifice of half their strength for no object whatev-

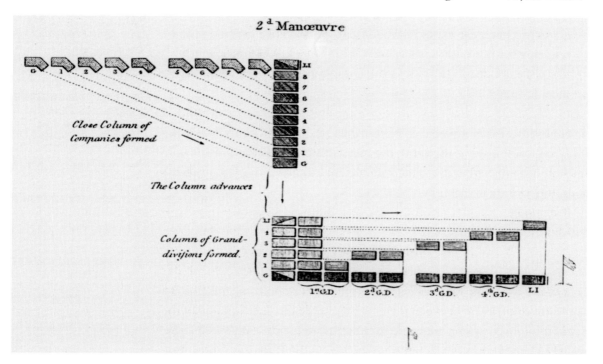

er'.[134] Conversely, Edward Macready observed of this unorthodox and presumably unpractised formation:

> In our condition at that time no power on earth could have formed a line of any kind out of us but that of a line four deep, by opening out from the centre of the rear face of the square, and wheeling up right and left, so indiscriminately were the men of all our companies mixed together, from closing in and replacing casualties in the front face. And even had we had time to have made our men step up and make a line two deep, we should have thereby lost the great advantage of retaining the power of wheeling back into square in a moment, which the nearness of the ridge, which we could not see over, rendered most advisable.[135]

A deeper formation could enable casualties in the first two ranks to be replaced from those in the third, but inevitably in action there was a contraction of a unit's frontage as men shuffled in towards the centre to fill the gaps, the 'closing in' described by Macready.

THE COLUMN

One of the enduring associations in the subject of Napoleonic infantry tactics is the comparison between the effectiveness of the line with that of the column, perhaps arising from the fact that many of the English-language sources concern the conflict between the two in the Peninsula. The association of the column with the French perhaps arises from their offensive use of it, though the subject is very much wider.

The term 'column' could be misinterpreted, if associated with the formation used on the march, in which the depth was very much greater than the frontage. The column used on the battlefield was entirely different, and was the standard formation for movement in all armies, a column being denser than a line and thus capable of more rapid movement without

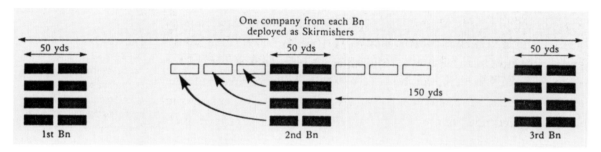

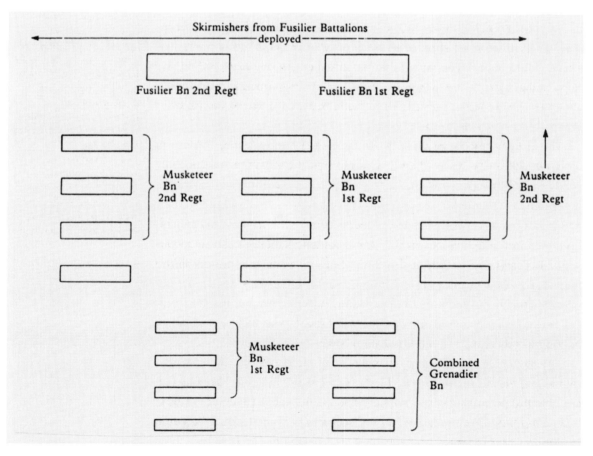

becoming disordered. Even in this sense, however, the term can cover a multitude of formations, up to large, densely packed bodies like the Austrian *Masse* to huge assemblies like that deployed by Marshal Macdonald at Wagram; indeed, it is possible to find columns confused with other formations in contemporary accounts, notably squares.

Although each army had its own drill, the basics of movement in column were fairly standard. For manoeuvre or combat it might have a frontage of one company, with the other companies of the battalion arrayed behind it; or with half that depth and a frontage of two companies, styled a 'column of divisions' (or in British service, sometimes 'grand divisions'), a 'division' in this sense being a tactical unit of two companies. An 'open column' was one in which there was manoeuvring-distance between the companies, a 'close column' one in which the companies followed one another in close proximity. Contrary to what might be imagined from the term, a column had a much wider frontage (in terms of men) than depth. For example, with the six-company battalion decreed for French infantry in 1808, with a strength of 120 men per company and with each company arrayed in three ranks, a 'column of divisions' would have a frontage of 40 men and a depth of 18 (excluding any deployed as skirmishers, when the depth would be reduced accordingly), and with the companies arrayed in two ranks the frontage would be even greater in proportion to the depth.

The French practice of delivering attacks in column was used from the early Revolutionary Wars, when it was said that the newly raised and only partly trained troops were unable to perform more complicated manoeuvres in line, so that columns served to keep them together and utilise their natural ardour in a rapid advance. There is some truth in this, but the column was not simply an expedient for half-trained recruits (linear tactics were also used successfully at this time), but was a vital component in the manoeuvres of all armies, though not all used it offensively with equal frequency. The effectiveness of French columns was perhaps emulated by others, however: for example, the Prussian 1812 regulations included an attack in column preceded by a screen of skirmishers.

Although able to move rapidly while retaining cohesion, the weakness of the column was in firepower. The most simplistic version of the 'line versus column' debate concerned the number of muskets each could bring to bear, and might be summarised by the scenario of an 800-strong battalion in column of divisions attacking an equal-sized unit in two-deep line.

A rare example of hand-to-hand combat in the open field: Sergeant Patrick Masterson of the British 87th captures the 'Eagle' of the French 8th Ligne at Barrosa by wresting it from Sous-Lieutenant Edmé Guillemaine, who was killed. Presumably having lost his spontoon, Masterson has resorted to using his sword. (Print after Clark & Dubourg.)

Whereas only the two front ranks of the column could fire (say 180 men), all 800 of those in line could fire upon the column. This point was emphasised by one of the exponents of the 'firepower' theory, Sir Charles Oman, in a lecture delivered to the Royal Artillery Institution in 1907, in which he compared the respective firepower of column and line 'pitted against each other with the beautiful simplicity that was witnessed at Maida'.[136] However valid the comparison, it was based on an incorrect premise, in that French sources make it clear that at Maida their troops were in line, which led Oman to revise his theory and state that it demonstrated instead the superiority of two-deep over three-deep line[137] (though the original text was subsequently reprinted unamended).[138]

If the firepower consideration were all that mattered, it would be surprising that French commanders persevered with an unsuccessful tactic (in Wellington's description, 'he moved forward in the old style, in columns, and was driven off in the old style'[139]). The reality was rather different, and concerns two important considerations. The first is that attack by column was ideally preceded by a horde of skirmishers and after the enemy line had been bombarded by artillery, so that the opposition might be wavering before the column even arrived within musket-range. Under these circumstances, the utility of the column 'is based on the *moral effect* produced on an enemy by the sight of masses advancing rapidly to charge', an effect so profound that the enemy often 'gave way whenever a French column *came within a certain distance of them*, and the French Generals never experienced much difficulty in *bringing up their columns to this critical point*.[140] To reinforce the effect on morale an advancing column might cheer; Suvarov reckoned it so important that 'Hurrah!' was forbidden unless ordered by at least a brigade-commander and it became a characteristic of Russian attacks (it was observed, for example, that when one was made by both Austrian and Russian troops at Austerlitz, it was the latter who cheered). It was equally true of French attacks, as described by a British witness: 'cheering and beating their drums, as if they had been going to scare crows from a corn-field ... Their officers too were in front of their men, waving their swords, and swaggering like showmen at a fair'.[141] (George Gleig described the 'discordant yell' of the French, 'a sort of shout, in which every man halloos for himself, without regard to the tone or time of those about him',[142] which he thought not half so intimidating as a concerted cheer.) The column may also have maintained the morale of those composing it, an Austrian commentator observing that the men in front knew they had supports in the rear, and those at the back felt safe by those in front forming what amounted to a parapet to absorb the enemy's shot; it was as if, he remarked, that fear formed columns, but courage deployed them.

The second consideration was in the maintenance of the column's formation. Where the enemy did not begin to waver and break before the approach of the column, some generals may deliberately have intended to press on in that formation. Gérard, for example, was criticised for purposely not attempting to deploy at Albuera, and a British witness of Barrosa recalled that 'we came within about twenty paces of them before they broke, and as they were in column, when they did they could not get away,

Left: French Imperial Guard in Spain, firing in line. Note how the second-rank men are taking muskets from those in the third, in the prescribed manner, while the front rank fires at will, so that loading, aiming and firing takes place in the same rank. (Engraving after Hippolyte Bellangé.)

Above: The advance of a French infantry column with successive companies formed in the classic three-deep method. (Print after Raffet.)

and it was therefore a scene of the most dreadful carnage'.[143] (Of this action, William Surtees noted 'they never yet got into line – nor did they intend, I believe – but advanced as a solid body, occasionally firing from their front'[144]). Otherwise, it is likely that most at least intended to deploy into line, to begin to exchange musketry, though it is possible that some of the accounts which suggest this occurred may have been witnessing spontaneous and unordered behaviour by the soldiers, rather than a deliberate tactic. Under heavy fire, however, it may have been impossible to get men to deploy: Edward Blakeney recalled how at Albuera he 'saw the French officers endeavouring to deploy their columns, but all to no purpose; for, as soon as a third of a company got out they immediately ran back, to be covered by the front of the column'[145] to escape the incoming fire. This is not a new point for discussion: as early as 1833 John Mitchell had remarked that French tactical experts were still discussing whether a column should be used for movement or action, which he observed was surprising in that they were still unaware of the actual purpose of a formation with which they had all but conquered Europe!

Another question was whether troops *should* stop to fire during the attack, as the loss of impetus might bring the advance to a halt and result in a bloody but indecisive musketry-duel, as occurred at Albuera. If such a halt occurred spontaneously, as is likely, it could cause other problems: Baron Lejeune, for example, claimed that when at Marengo the leading Austrian battalions halted to fire at Desaix's approach, those in the rear failed to halt 'so as to maintain their proper distance for manoeuvring, all pressed on in confusion, till it was quite impossible for them to deploy'[146] and chaos

Above: A French infantry column of attack, at Moucroen (29 April 1794). (Print after Mozin.)

ensued. (The Austrian regulations of 1798 specified that in an advance in line a unit should halt sixty paces from an enemy, fire, then continue to quickmarch, muskets at the 'recover' position, then halt *again* before levelling the muskets and charging.) It was stated that the British attacks at Bergen-op-Zoom and New Orleans failed because the troops halted to fire instead of pushing on, and there was much discussion at the time on the need to storm a defended position without firing – 'the absurdity of firing at stone walls' was quoted[147] – which certainly occurred. It was also stated that fire from an advancing line was so inaccurate that it caused more disruption in the advancing unit than it did to the enemy.[148] Advocates of the 'no firing' advance included Maurice de Saxe and Scharnhorst, and the case of Hochkirch was also quoted, when Austrian troops had halted to fire and then begun file-firing, which once begun was difficult to stop, thus causing a considerable delay during which the Prussians were able to reorganise.

One commentator remarked that the reason why naval landing-parties so often stormed positions successfully was because many of the sailors were not armed with muskets, so *had* to rush on. There were cases where soldiers were prevented from firing and thus compelled to charge forward. One of the classic examples occurred in General Charles Grey's attack upon 'Mad Anthony' Wayne's command at Paoli (September 1777), made with flints removed to ensure the speed of the attack (giving rise to the nick-

Above: An attack by infantry in column preceded by troops thrown forward as skirmishers: French troops at Pérulle (April 1793). (Print after A. Rochu.)

name 'No-Flint Grey'); but there were many other incidents of flints being removed or, as at Montmirail, when Ney ordered the Imperial Guard to charge having first shaken the priming powder from their pans. It was also stated as an encouragement to rush on, that with a maximum effective rate of fire of three shots per minute and with no sensible officer opening fire at more than 100 yards, only one volley could be delivered as troops without packs could cover that distance in twenty seconds; and by firing at will, and not by volley, 'you might as well seek to put out a fire with a watering-pot, as to stop an out-and-out rush'.[149]

William Napier wrote of the sensations of attacking in column, praising the formation for manoeuvre and emphasising the point about knowing when to deploy:

> The column is undoubtedly excellent for all movements short of the actual charge, but as the Macedonian phalanx was unable to resist the open formation of the Roman legion, so will the close column be unequal to sustain the fire and charge of a good line aided by artillery. The natural repugnance of men to trample on their own dead and wounded, the cries and groans of the latter, and the whistling of the cannon-shots as they tear open the ranks, produce the greatest disorder, especially in the centre of attacking columns which blinded by

smoke, unstedfast [*sic*] of footing, and bewildered by words of command coming from a multitude of officers crowded together, can neither see what is taking place, nor make any effort to advance or retreat without increasing the confusion: no example of courage can be useful, no moral effect can be produced by the spirit of individuals, except upon the head, which is often firm, and even victorious at the moment the rear is flying in terror. Nevertheless, well managed columns are the very soul of military operations, in them is the victory, and in them also is safety to be found after a defeat. The secret consists in knowing when and where to extend the front.[150]

Column v. line: in this depiction of the action at Boussu (3 November 1792) a French column can be seen charging towards an Austrian line (background); the Austrians are delivering fire by volley but the line is already beginning to waver at the approach of the column, which is supported on the flanks by artillery. (Print after Hippolyte Lecomte.)

This also emphasises the vulnerability of the column to artillery fire, as roundshot would scythe down as many men as stood in its path, and by hitting a column, especially obliquely, would cause terrible damage. An Austrian writer, for example, compared columns to butts for artillery practice, and some witnesses left graphic accounts of columns thus hit. Major Sempronius Stretton of the British 40th, for example, recalled how his battalion was struck when in column at Waterloo, a single shot decapitating Captain William Fisher and ploughing on to strike down more than twenty-five men, 'the most destructive shot I ever witnessed during a long period of service'.[151] Several accounts of the same battle describe how the Imperial

Guard was lashed by artillery fire in its advance, the columns wavering, 'at each successive discharge, like standing corn blown by the wind',[152] the dark mass of men revealing 'long lanes of light ... seen through the black body'[153] as ranks were struck down.

If the attack – whether delivered in column or line – did not pause to fire but pushed on, it might be expected that a bayonet-fight would ensue; but this happened on only the rarest of occasions, for just as it was not necessary for a musket to hit an individual at 100 yards, so it was not necessary for a bayonet to be blooded, if the sight of it caused the enemy to flee. A number of commentators expressed a common belief:

> Although these columns of attack were set in motion with the sole view of breaking through the opposing lines, or shattering at the point of the bayonet the adverse columns against which they were directed, a charge with this weapon, such as is commonly understood, where bayonet crosses bayonet in the 'tug of war', is a thing which has never been known, except partially, or where a dense smoke has brought troops unconsciously close upon each other. It has never taken place premeditatedly, or to the extent of a whole corps being thus engaged; because either one or the other party has invariably given way before an actual contact has taken place, and when the victors have only had to strike at flying men ... It has always been the same where column has been opposed to column – *the contest is merely a moral one* – for long before they meet, one wavers – halts – and is lost. It is a contest of which the decision is influenced by the greater resolution displayed by one or other of the adverse bodies.[154]

The bayonet was, in effect, the supreme psychological weapon, even though it might cause few casualties. William Napier compared its efficacy to bathing in a river, remarking that in the rapid and dangerous Rhône few people were ever drowned because few ventured into it, while in the slow-moving Saône many were lost, and so with the bayonet: so few were killed by it as so few dared to stand and face it. To use a French expression quoted at the time, victory at close quarters went to those who preserved *la meilleure contenance*. Troops confident of using the bayonet would advance; those fearful of its consequences were more likely to turn aside: as a participant in the fight at Garris in the Pyrenees in February 1814 stated, the bayonet's 'power consists in numbers, acting together as one machine in a closed compact line', with the troops having 'the very highest confidence in it; and marched to the attack fully determined to use it ... and the enemy knew that [they] would do so'.[155] Indeed, those with confidence might prefer to advance to close quarters rather than stand to be shot at: as one officer remarked, those who withstood a galling fire would hear 'a low whisper run amongst the men of "I wish they would let us give them the steel"; or "Let us give them the *Brummagem*"',[156] (a colloquialism for 'Birmingham', where steel was produced). Such a desire sometimes had to be checked: Thomas Austin recalled how, at Merxem in 1814, his company received a volley (fired high) at twenty paces, which did little harm but caused the men spontaneously to fix bayonets and prepare to charge. This was checked by the officers who ordered 'Right about face! Order arms! Unfix bayonets!'[157] so that the men were brought to order with backs to the enemy; only then were they faced-about and began to deliver orderly musketry, advancing merely when reinforced.

The effect on morale of the sight of an approaching line of bayonets was described by William Grattan in his account of the advance of Wallace's brigade at Salamanca. As they advanced they received a destructive volley but moved on before the smoke had cleared so that their French opponents could not see its dire effect. The French appeared astounded that the advance had not been stopped:

> Nevertheless they opened a heavy discharge of musketry, but it was unlike the former – it was irregular and ill-directed, the men acted without concert or method, and many fired in the air. At length their fire ceased altogether, and the three [British] regiments, for the first time, *cheered*! The effect was electric; Foy's troops were seized with a panic, and as Wallace closed upon them, his men could distinctly remark their bearing. Their mustachioed faces, one and all, presented the same ghastly hue, a horrid family likeness throughout; and as they stood to receive the shock ... they reeled to and fro like men intoxicated. The French officers did all that was possible, by voice, gesture, and example, to rouse their men to a proper sense of their situation, but in vain ... the mighty phalanx, which but a moment before was so formidable, loosened and fell in pieces ... Wallace, seeing the terrible confusion that prevailed in the enemy's column, pressed on with his brigade, calling to his soldiers 'to push on to the muzzle'.[158]

Line v. column: encouraged by its officers, a French column approaches a British line, which is holding its fire until the last moment. Note the colour-sergeant (left) armed with a spontoon. (Print after Richard Simkin.)

To compel the troops to hold their fire in this advance, the British officers had marched ahead of the line.

It was said that the difference between troops retiring before musketry was different from before bayonets:

> Men dispersed by fire retire slowly, lose nothing of their self-confidence, and once rallied and brought to see the really trifling effect of fire ... ever after under-value its real power. Charged with the bayonet, however, they must disperse at full speed, or perish ... unless very desperate, they will always fly; and men who have once shrunk from personal conflict will always feel a considerable degree of awe and reverence for those from whom they fled. Any man, woman, or child can pull a trigger, but none except brave and highly excited men will meet their opponents with the cold steel.[159]

It is more likely that prolonged fights became see-saw combats, with one side retiring temporarily before an advance, then returning to the attack as the other side withdrew, without hand-to-hand combat ever developing; at Austerlitz the action at the village of Pratzen may have been such a case, with French troops retiring before a Russian bayonet-charge, and then the reverse when the French were reinforced. As one commentator remarked, what was termed a charge was often no more than an advance following musketry.

Because of the prevalence of English contemporary accounts, much of the assessment of lines and columns has centred upon the defeat of French columns by British lines in the Peninsula, which can give only an incomplete picture of the utilisation of the two formations in general. These combats were decided by a British tactic which appears to have been reproduced only rarely by other armies: of deploying a line upon the reverse slope of a ridge and thus hidden from the view of the attackers. This gave the defenders a dual advantage: when they did appear from behind the brow of the hill the attackers would be startled at their proximity, and also would have no time to deploy, if indeed that had been their intention. Furthermore, the British did not engage in a long musketry-duel, but generally delivered only one massive volley and then counter-charged. This could shatter the morale of the attackers. The later French commentator, Colonel C. J. J. J. Ardant du Picq, remarked that the impetus and boost to morale conveyed by an offensive movement would be more than offset by the good order of the defenders and the greater losses that the attackers might expect to sustain, so that any offensive reaction from the defenders would both disorganise and demoralise the attack. This, he thought, was the secret of the British success in the Peninsula.

The Marquis de Chambray described such an advance from the viewpoint of one involved in the attack:

> The French infantry … charges … with shouldered arms … deployed or in close columns of divisions; it has often succeeded against the

The counter-charge against an attacking column: British infantry repel an attack at Busaco. (Print after T. St Clair.)

Austrians and other troops, who begin firing at too great a distance; but it has always failed against the English, who only open their fire within a short distance ... In order to defend a height, the English infantry does not crown the crest, as is practised by the infantry of other armies; it is placed about fifty yards behind the crest, a position in which it is not to be seen if the ascent be at all steep; it has almost always some skirmishers along the slope, which must be climbed in order to attack it. The musketry and the retreat of the skirmishers inform it of the enemy's arrival; at the moment that they appear it gives them a discharge of musketry, the effect of which must be terrible at so short a distance, and charges them immediately. If it succeeds in overthrowing them, which is very probable, it is satisfied with following with its skirmishers ... and resumes its position ... It can easily be imagined that a body which charges another, and which is itself charged, after having received a fire which has carried destruction and disorder into its ranks, must necessarily be overthrown.

He then quoted Talavera as an example, where:

The French charged with shouldered arms, according to their custom. Being arrived at a short distance and the English line remaining immobile, the soldiers hesitated to advance. The officers and non-commissioned officers cried to the soldiers: 'Forward – march – do not fire!' – some of them even exclaimed 'They surrender!' Then they continued their forward movement, and were very near the English line, when it opened a fire of two ranks, which carried destruction into the French line, stopped its progress, and produced some disorder. While the officers cried to the soldiers, 'Forward, do not fire!' and the fire had commenced notwithstanding all their efforts, the English, leaving off fire, charged with the bayonet. Every circumstance was favourable to them – good order – the impulse given – the determination to fight with the bayonet: among the French, on the contrary, no longer an impulse – the surprise occasioned by the unexpected resolution of the enemy – disorder – they had no alternative but flight. Their flight, however, was not the result of fear, but necessity.

Citing the action at Sorauren, Chambray described how the French advanced in close column of divisions:

From time to time the English officers came to examine at what point the French columns had arrived. As soon as they appeared, the English battalions fired, charged with the bayonet, and overthrew them, but did not pursue [but] retired in double quick time. Nevertheless, the French division, of which the first ranks only had attained the plateau, astonished at being repulsed, almost without having fought, rallied immediately, and re-ascended the hill with great resolution [but] were again charged and overthrown.[160]

The fact that the emotional energy of the French must have peaked before the counter-charge, while the British troops' feelings had been kept in check, must have been crucial. Where it could be seen (as described in a famous passage describing a French attack, by Thomas Bugeaud),[161] the absolute stillness of the British line, contrasting with the noise and agitation of the French, must have been unnerving to the attackers. The fire, wrote Bugeaud, hit the column like a thunderbolt, and before they could recover their equilibrium the British cheered (more severe intimidation) and immediately advanced with levelled bayonets.

This counter-charge was the standard practice, as ordered by Colonel Alexander Wallace of the British 88th at Busaco: 'When I bring you face to face with those French rascals, drive them down the hill – don't give them the false touch, but push home to the muzzle!'[162] Edward Macready observed: 'All firing beyond one volley in a case where you must charge, seems only to cause an [sic] useless interchange of casualties, besides endangering the steadiness of a charge to be undertaken in the midst of a sustained file fire, when a word of command must be hard to hear.'[163] Such charges were intentionally very limited: as Moyle Sherer overheard Wellington order at Busaco: 'If they attempt this point again, Hill, you will give them a volley and charge bayonets: but don't let your people follow them too far down the hill.'[164] These actions did not necessarily produce many casualties if the attackers gave way at the very sight of the counter-charge; one witness of Maida, for example, remarked that most of the French casualties had wounds in their back, and it was remarked that most of these had occurred only because a dry water-course had hindered their withdrawal, where they were overtaken by the pursuing British.

The rapid advance with the bayonet, immediately after firing, was not a new tactic: in 1727 Humphrey Bland had noted that a unit should reserve its fire to close range and then fall upon the enemy:

The counter-charge against an attack: British infantry (right) repel French troops at Maida.

With the bayonets on the muzzles the instant [you] have fired, which may be done under the cover of the smoke, before they can perceive it; so that by the shock they will receive from your fire, by being close, and attacking them immediately with your bayonets, they may, in all probability, be beat with a very inconsiderable loss: but if you do not follow your fire that moment, but give them time to recover from the disorder yours may have put them into, the scene may change to your disadvantage.[165]

Without the psychological advantage of the 'reverse slope' tactic, however, at times attacks could only be pressed with difficulty. For example, George Gleig recorded the action around Handaye near the Bidassoa in 1813, in which a British column advanced, their French opponents firing and then retreating until rallied by a bold officer. The British deployed into line and received another volley, which shook them so much that 'it was not without considerable difficulty, and after having exchanged with them several volleys, that we succeeded in getting within charging distance'. As they cheered the French again broke, and as the bold officer again began to rally them he was shot dead; 'the fall of that man decided the day',[166] and the French fled.

This implies that it was difficult to get even steady troops to advance against persistent musketry, and that only when the psychological balance tipped was the action decided, rather different from the concept of one side or the other rushing on irresistibly. What constituted 'charging distance' is not stated, but it is perhaps significant that at Castrillo in 1812, when Anson's brigade charged Brennier's division, which broke when the attackers were within fifty or sixty paces, it was said that having begun the charge too soon the men were so disordered and out of breath that they could hardly use their bayonets![167]

At the time, it was believed that the ability to stand up to an attack was the result of national characteristics: 'The French people never closed on the Saxon-English ... the Swedes, the Americans, the Turks, if uni-Italianized, and our own mutinous population, are the only enemies now who will wait a bayonet-shock'[168] ('mutinous population' refers to the then recent fight with the rebels of 'Mad Tom' Courteney at Bossenden in Kent). Others emphasised discipline and morale, as Napier remarked of the French, whose 'habitual method of attacking in column cannot be praised. Against the Austrians, Russians, and Prussians, it may have been successful, but against the British it must always fail; because the English infantry is sufficiently firm, intelligent, and well disciplined, to wait calmly in lines for the adverse masses, and sufficiently bold to close upon them with the bayonet.'[169]

Others cited what might be termed the 'courage of the mass', not present in individuals but formed by discipline and the ability to act in concert, 'an aggregation of comparative cowards, united into a strong and daring body' which could sweep away hosts of heroic warriors devoid of order or discipline. It was said that the Russian soldier exemplified the point: not inherently aggressive and treated by his superiors worse than the soldiers of almost any other army, yet quite unshakeable in his determination to do his duty: 'He will stand passively to be cut to pieces, or he will advance as he is directed; his arm may be unnerved, indeed, by his individual terrors, but still he *keeps his place* – the man is there, at his post, forming part and parcel of *a brave and formidable whole* – a whole which stands unawed by danger, or which itself advances threatening.' The result, it was said, was marked: 'The French, if they repulsed and out-manoeuvred them, and carried their positions, displaying everywhere the superiority of their fiery courage and of their martial talent, could yet, in the full tide of success, obtain few of those marked and decisive victories which signalised their contests with the Germans.'[170]

Clausewitz commented on the merits of hand-to-hand fighting as opposed to longer-range musketry. The former, he noted, was invariably destructive, so that one side or the other would attempt to escape from it, whereas the enemy's destruction was less certain with musketry. The logical progression from this would be that the more deadly form of combat was actually less so, if one side soon ran to escape it, while the less lethal form might prove the opposite, if troops stood to exchange fire without breaking. Despite what appears to have been the overwhelming psychological effect of the bayonet, there were occasions when troops did stand to fight hand-to-hand. Many of these occurred in the defence of villages, or of fieldworks like those at Borodino. Others occurred under peculiar conditions, including cases where one side just could not get away. One of the few detailed accounts of a bayonet-fight, for example, was recounted by a member of the British 71st in the Peninsula, who recalled how his comrades were attacked by French troops while sheltering behind a wall, and how they only stood to await the attack because escape was impossible, having a muddy, ploughed field at their back. (The French were driven off after a 'pell-mell' fight in which the writer had to bayonet an opponent, who was fighting mad and refused to be taken prisoner.)

Baron Lejeune described another reason why troops might not retreat, in his account of what he considered a very exceptional encounter, a mêlée 'such as is very rare in modern warfare, for as a rule one of the corps engaged is demoralised, to begin with, by the firing, and draws back before the enemy is near enough to cross muzzles'; but at Barrosa, 'our non-commissioned officers, placed as a supernumerary rank, crossed their muskets behind their squads, thus forming buttresses which kept the ranks from giving way'. He noted how furious such fights might be by remarking that 'when the English had broken their weapons by striking with butt or bayonet, they ... went on fighting with their fists'.[171]

Even where both sides were unshaken, 'irregularities in the ground, waverings in the line, or the two lines, on closing, happening to be inclined and not parallel to each other, have probably prevented more than a few files from coming into close conflict at any one point. These would use their bayonets; but the others being obliged to conform to their line, and not being near enough to fight with the bayonet, would soon naturally resort to firing.'[172]

Some of the recorded close-quarter fights occurred virtually by accident, such as that at Roncesvalles, which was held to be one of the few genuine bayonet-combats of some duration, in the open field and unaccompanied by musketry, during the entire period. Captain George Tovey's light company of the British 20th Foot was clearing French skirmishers from a plateau when they were suddenly confronted by the head of the 6th Léger which had ascended the slope unseen, and to the amazement of all concerned:

> My company absolutely paused in astonishment, for we were face to face with them ... I repeated, 'Bayonet away! – Bayonet away!' and, rushing headlong amongst them, we fairly turned them back into the descent of the hill; and such was the panic and confusion occasioned amongst them by our sudden onset, that this small party – for small it was compared to the French column – had time to regain the regiment ... The company ... did not amount to more than between seventy and eighty men, and we had eleven killed and fourteen wounded. ... A powerful man by the name of Budworth returned with only the blood-soiled socket of the bayonet on his piece, and he declared that he had killed away until his bayonet broke; and I am confident, from the reckless and intrepid nature of the man, that he had done so.[173]

A formation which sought to combine the best features of both line and column was *l'ordre mixte*, which supposedly originated during the French Revolutionary Wars: a battalion in line with a battalion in column on each flank to execute a rapid advance while covered by the fire of the centre. The formation could be employed up to divisional level, and may have originated with the French infantry

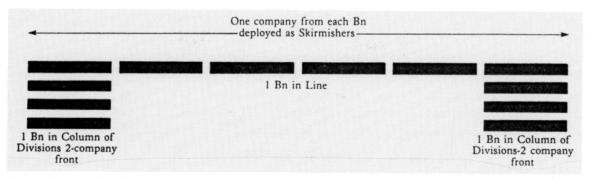

One company from each Bn
deployed as Skirmishers

1 Bn in Line

1 Bn in Column of
Divisions 2-company
front

1 Bn in Column of
Divisions-2 company
front

Above: The principle of l'ordre mixte, involving battalions of nine companies each, each block representing a 'division' of two companies.

Left: A depiction of the principle of l'ordre mixte: French infantry charge Austro-Hungarian troops (left and foreground) while others in line provide covering fire, at Thionville, October 1792). (Print after Hippolyte Lecomte.)

reorganisation of 1793–4, the *amalgame*, which associated one regular battalion (capable of delivering disciplined musketry) with two newly formed battalions, the limited training of which made them most suited for a rush forward in column. This classic *ordre mixte*, however, may have been employed on relatively few occasions, and rather than being an innovation may have been no more than a progression of earlier tactical theories which sensibly allowed battalion columns to deploy, or not, according to circumstances. *L'ordre mixte* may also have been confused with a heavy skirmishline preceding an attack in column. Although its devising has been ascribed to Napoleon – probably without clear evidence – the concept of securing the flanks of a line with units in column or square was a common expedient, defensive in origin (to protect the vulnerable flanks from attack, notably by cavalry) rather than as with Napoleon's classic *ordre mixte* offensive. It was used by the Russians, for example, and instances may be found in British service, such as at Castrillo (18 July 1812) when the two battalions of Anson's Brigade of the 4th Division advanced in line, with Stubbs's Portuguese brigade in column on the flanks. An example of the same practice virtually on the scale of the classic French *ordre mixte* was described by Robert Knowles of the British 7th Fuzileers concerning the covering of Wellington's retreat from Fuente Guinaldo in 1811, when: 'Our Regiment advanced in line with the 23rd and 48th in close column on each flank.'[174]

THE SQUARE

Just as the term 'column' covered a range of formations, such was also the case with 'the square', the universal defence against an attack by cavalry. An oblong or rectangle of men, facing outwards, its defence was both by musketry and by presenting a phalanx of fixed bayonets against which a horse could not be made to rush. The formation of squares, however, was considerably more complex than this popular perception.

One of the most basic varieties was the 'solid square' which could be formed by no more complicated manoeuvre than simply closing-up the ranks of a column, with the files on the flanks facing outwards and those at the rear facing about. This must have especially useful for troops of limited training and experience who might lack the discipline to form a hollow square quickly when under attack, for the conversion from column to solid square could probably be accomplished at considerable speed. It was used by many armies, French and British included, but perhaps the best-known variation was the *Masse* formation employed by the Austrians. There were two principal forms of *Masse*: *Bataillonsmasse*, one company wide and six deep, and *Divisionsmasse*, two companies wide and three deep; but the use of this version of a solid formation did not preclude the hollow square, which was also used. In Prussian service, though, a similar formation was decreed by the 1812 regulations as the universal defence against cavalry, replacing the hollow square. Solid squares formed from basically closed-up columns, however, had little room for manoeuvre, and were criticised as being 'encumbered by their density of formation, and yet not at all more difficult of attack in respect of the quantity of fire they are able to oppose to cavalry',[175] as while such a formation would keep its members from being ridden down, only two or three ranks on each side would be able to fire. It is likely, though, that the very sensible priority of security took precedence over the damage which could be inflicted upon the enemy in such desperate circumstances. (Some may have thought the type of defensive formation depended upon the nature of the enemy: Suvarov, for example, stated that squares should always be employed against Turks, but columns against the French.)

The hollow square was formed either from line or column, usually by the wheeling of companies or sub-companies. Each army had its own drill, but the circumstances under which it was formed in combat were common to all, as Alexander Wallace told his 88th Foot: 'Mind the square; you know I often told you that if ever you had to form it from line, in the face of an enemy, you'd be in a d—d ugly way, and have plenty of noise about you ... by G-d, if once you are broken, you'll be running here and there like a parcel of *frightened pullets*!'[176] In essence, the hollow square was a rectangular formation with a number of ranks in each face (commonly three or four), facing outwards, with space inside for officers, musicians, Colours and casu-

Right: The British system of forming a hollow square from line, and the methods of marching in square, from Dickinson's Instructions for Forming a Regiment of Infantry, 1798.

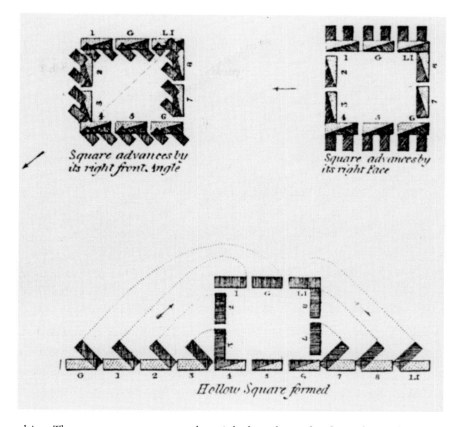

Right: The British system of forming a hollow square from line, and the methods of marching in square, from Dickinson's Instructions for Forming a Regiment of Infantry, 1798.

alties. The outer one or two ranks might kneel, musket-butts braced against the ground, with bayonets angled towards horses'-breast height, producing an almost impregnable hedge of steel. The kneeling position, however, was criticised as being potentially unstable, as demonstrated by a parlour-game called *l'Exercise Prussienne*, in which a young lady would order the rest of the company to perform various manoeuvres, and end by having them kneel down in this manner, in line, whereupon the lady would push the one on the end and the whole lot would topple over. (Austrian practice, for example, was to have squares three-deep, the first rank standing and reserving its fire for very close range, the second rank standing to fire at longer range, and the third standing to load muskets for the second.) A French commentator noted that standing to aim bayonets at a horse's head, as they did in Egypt, was more successful than aiming at breast-height, which tended to infuriate the horses and cause them to lash out with their hooves, as was observed against the Russians at Austerlitz.

The term 'square' can be misleading as the formation might be oblong; in fact Dundas's British manual refers throughout to 'the square or oblong'. The

shape of a square often depended upon the number of sub-units it contained, so that a battalion of ten companies might have three companies in the front and rear faces, and two on the sides, although the British regulations also mentioned a 'perfect' square of two companies per side, with the two flank companies standing in reserve at the rear (which would presumably also apply if one or more companies were deployed as skirmishers). In the field, when squares had to be formed with great speed, variations from the regulation drill may not have been unknown. At Waterloo, for example, the British 3rd Division was formed into oblongs with front and rear faces of four companies in strength, the sides of but one company, at the behest of Captain James Shaw,[177] who, as Assistant Quartermaster-General, was entrusted with its deployment. Following unfortunate incidents at Quatre Bras, he was anxious to eliminate delays in the formation of a square, observing of his new disposition that 'when a battalion forms oblong in this manner upon the two centre companies, the formation is made in *less* than half the time in which it would form square on a flank company'.[178] He also emphasised the value of aligning squares in chequerboard fashion, so that their musketry would not strike an adjacent square; he achieved this at Waterloo by simply assembling his battalions in two lines, initially in column, with those of the second line facing the intervals between the battalions in the first line. A French alternative was to align squares with a corner facing the enemy, so that when the faces of the square fired to their front, the shots would not strike the adjacent square on the same lateral axis.

The square: perhaps the most famous of all portrayals, Lady Elizabeth Butler's 'Quatre Bras'. This shows a corner of a square; note the officer behind the third rank, directing fire by pointing his sword. (Print after Lady Butler.)

A square under attack: British infantry at Waterloo assailed by French cuirassiers, which have approached within sword-range, something which was recorded as occurring at that battle. (Print after P. Jazet.)

British hollow squares were normally formed four deep, but the regulations mentioned squares of two, three and six ranks deep, according to circumstances. For example, the three-deep square was used at El Hamet in 1807, as there is particular mention of those wounded who were able to kneel, and non-combatants being armed, forming 'a fourth or supernumerary rank with[in] the square.'[179] In action, the haste with which squares might be formed could result in non-regulation formations; for example, Edward Macready recalled how his battalion formed square with such urgency at Quatre Bras that two faces were six-deep, and thus capable of delivering a 'tremendous' volley. Other accounts note that, from haste of formation or by the transfer of men from one face to replace the casualties in another, companies would become 'mixed in one irregular mass – grenadier, light, and battalion companies' together, so that precise, drill-ground manoeuvres would have been quite impossible, and that thereafter squares would have to be formed 'so far as unequalised companies could form a square'.[180]

Despite the nature of the square's formation, musketry remained a vital component, as emphasised by the 1798 Austrian regulations for example. These stressed the need to remain 'cool and collected' and to realise that security depended less upon firing than upon reserving fire until it was certain to take effect. As the enemy cavalry approached, they stated, the square should 'present', which in itself might be sufficient to cause the cavalry to turn aside, in which case the square should bring down its muskets and reserve its fire for a genuine threat. John Mitchell concurred, stating that it was possible to fire only once at a cavalry charge, for to attempt to load after the first volley would produce an unsteadiness in the square which would be fatal.

Although terribly vulnerable to artillery-fire, in all but exceptional circumstances a square was impregnable to cavalry attack, provided that its members kept their nerve. The serried ranks of bayonets were fatally intimidating to any trooper's hope of riding his horse into them, and another factor in its strength was the relatively small size, so that only a limited number of cavalry could attack it. Thus it was remarked that it was immaterial whether sixty or seventy cavalry made an attack (the average number which could hope to close with a square because of its limited frontage), or 600–700: the chance of breaking the square was the same. Against them, a square could deliver a considerable volume of musketry: one of the advantages of the hollow over the solid square was said to be the greater 'supply of fire' while still maintaining sufficient solidity.

A cavalry officer remarked:

Breaking a square is a thing thing never heard of. The infantry either break before the cavalry come up, or they drive them back with their fire. It is an awful thing for infantry to see a body of cavalry riding at them full gallop. The men in the square frequently begin to shuffle, and so create some unsteadiness. This causes them to neglect their fire. The cavalry, seeing them waver, have an inducement for riding

A well-formed square would stand out amid the chaos of battle: the last stand of the French Old Guard at Waterloo. (Print after Raffet.)

close up, and in all probability succeed in getting into the square, when all is over. When once broken, the infantry, of course, have no chance. If steady, it is almost impossible to succeed against infantry, yet I should always be cautious, if in command of infantry attacked by cavalry, having seen the best troops more afraid of cavalry than any other force.[181]

This explains exhortations like that of Francis Skelly Tidy to his inexperienced 3/14th Foot at Waterloo: 'Now, my young tinkers, stand firm! While you remain in your present position, old Harry himself can't touch you; but if *one* of you give way, *he* will have every mother's son of you, as sure as you are born!'[182] Of the relatively few cases of squares being broken by cavalry alone, it would seem that the unsteadiness of the infantry left them already half defeated, but troops could be steadied again. The most exposed parts of a square, presumably requiring the most reliable men, were the corners; at Waterloo, for example, Edward Cotton recalled that 'it was quite amusing to see some of the foreign troops cut away from the angles of their squares, and our staff-officers galloping after them to intercept their flight. It was surprising to see how readily they returned to their squares.'[183]

Except under unusual circumstances (some detailed in the companion title *Napoleonic Weapons and Warfare: Cavalry*), the cavalry's best hope of defeating a square, unless the infantry were fatally unsteady, was to fall upon it before the square had been completed. This occurred, for example, at Quatre Bras, when as the British 69th Foot was preparing to receive a cavalry charge, Major Henry Lindsey ordered three companies to face about and open fire, with the result that the square was not closed and the battalion was ridden down and lost a Colour: 'Poor man, to the day of his death he regretted having done so, but at the time he did it for the best.'[184] During the same battle the British 42nd closed their square but in the process trapped some French cavalry inside, who were quickly despatched.

During a long action, a unit might form square and revert to line on any number of occasions, and although a solid column was preferable for movement, even a hollow square could march in that formation, with either a face or a corner leading. Marmont noted that it was not to be recommended as liable to cause disorder from inequalities of terrain and the fact that some men were marching in file and others in line. Nevertheless, an example of how well a square could manoeuvre was demonstrated by the British 79th at Toulouse. While advancing, the battalion commander, Lieutenant-Colonel

A 'rallying square' – an ad hoc knot of men formed under the most desperate of circumstances, as in this illustration of British infantry attacked by French hussars. (Print after Vereker M. Hamilton.)

Neil Douglas, noticed the approach of cavalry, so formed square and ordered Ensign Jeremiah Balfour with a Colour to precede it, to indicate the direction of advance. 'Balfour's conduct was much admired; he carried himself quite erect, the colours inclined forward, which as he had no shoulder or waist belt to support them required strength of arm, pointed his toes, and gave the step to the square with as much regularity and correctness as he would have done at any formal parade in England'.[185] When within range, Douglas called in the ensign and ordered his grenadiers to deliver a volley, whereupon the cavalry turned around and slowly rode off with as much composure as they had advanced, evidently with neither side suffering a casualty. Under combat conditions, the pace of a square and column were probably similar: for example, at El Bodon a square formed by the British 5th and 77th retreated with admirable precision, in the face of heavy attack, while the accompanying Portuguese 21st marched alongside in solid 'close column', opening up only to by-pass the casualties after a shell dropped into its midst.

Some believed that infantry in line could resist cavalry (Harry Smith, for example, certainly did[186]), though when this did occur it caused some comment (as with the Chasseurs Britanniques at Fuentes de Oñoro, although they were apparently behind a stone wall). There were cases of a unit facing its rear rank about to deal with an attack from behind: perhaps the best-known example concerns the British 28th at Alexandria (the origin of the 'back badge' worn in commemoration by the Gloucestershire Regiment[187]), but this was not a unique occurrence: at Marengo, for example, the French 72nd was charged simultaneously in front and rear, and its rear rank (of three) turned about to drive off the enemy. It was even said that a single infantryman with musket and bayonet, if he kept his nerve, could keep most cavalrymen at bay, if only because the latter had to be as expert a horseman as a swordsman before he could hope to deliver a telling blow.

This factor must have counted in the formation of a 'rallying square', in which skirmishers or members of a broken unit would run to an officer or NCO and form a knot around him, producing a miniature version of a solid square (the German term was the rather appropriate *Klumpen* ('clump' or 'lump'). George Gleig recalled an incident in the Peninsula:

> There was no time to collect or form a square, so we threw ourselves as best we could into compact circles, and stood to receive them. They came on with the noise of thunder. One circle wavered – some of the men abandoned their ranks – the cavalry rode through it in an instant. That in which I was stood more firm. We permitted them to approach till the breasts of the horses almost touched our bayonets, when a close and well-directed volley was poured in, and numbers fell beneath it.'[188]

The way in which even a small number of men could resist a cavalry attack was demonstrated in an exercise which got out of hand in Australia in 1860. After their captain had been hit in the face by a blank round, the sixty-strong Kyneton troop of cavalry lost their temper with a twenty-two-man rallying-square of the Maryborough Volunteers and for ten minutes tried to break it, injuring one man and attacking with such violence that one of the troopers broke his sabre. Nevertheless, the square remained steady, only one man rising from the crouch (and that with the intent of attacking the cavalryman whose blows he was parrying with his musket); he was restrained by his sergeant so hard that his coat tore. This action, which won the victorious infantry the nickname of 'the Iron Square', demonstrates what could be achieved by a small group of determined men, and the result would have been even more marked had they been able to fire live rounds.[189]

A remarkable incident where that actually occurred concerned the grenadier company of the French 22nd *Ligne*, which at Villar de Puerco in July 1810 was attacked by cavalry while reconnoitring. Despite the small numbers, they formed a perfectly viable square, and under the inspirational leadership of Captain Gouache and Sergeant Patois, beat off two charges and discouraged a third, inflicted twenty-four casualties and suffered none. Gouache began file-firing at thirty yards' range, and the cavalry approached so close that they were able to cut at the bayonets.

The square was also used for larger tactical formations, as adopted by Napoleon in Egypt, as a counter to the rapid attacks of the Mameluke cavalry. Perhaps inspired by Austrian and Russian practice in combat against the Turks, the French formed huge divisional squares, with artillery at the corners and protected by light infantry, with sufficient space in the hollow interior to accommodate the sick, non-combatants and baggage. These formations were used both for combat and for movement. Marmont noted that they were initially formed with the 'almost ridiculous' depth of six ranks, but that experience led them to reduce this to three or even two ranks deep. Squares of such large size could be more vulnerable than the compact battalion square: for example, Mendizabel formed his Spanish infantry into huge divisional squares at the Gebora (1811), but they were swept away by a dual attack by infantry and cavalry. (This emphasised the crucial importance of co-ordination of 'arms': if attacking cavalry were accompanied by artillery, their infantry opponents would have to remain in square or risk being ridden down, but the square presented such a target that they could quite literally be slaughtered once the guns opened fire.) Nevertheless, the effectiveness of the larger square, with space in the centre to shelter casualties and supplies, led to its use in colonial campaigns throughout the nineteenth century.

Infantry in line drive off cavalry, the front rank in the 'prepare to receive cavalry' position: Sir Charles Belson and the British 28th Foot at Quatre Bras. (Print after George Jones.)

NOTES

The sources of quotations listed in the footnotes refer to titles which appear in the Bibliography. The following abbreviations are used to identify contemporary publications:

BML: *British Military Library or Journal*
CUSM: *Colburn's United Service Magazine*
USJ: *United Service Journal*
USM: *United Service Magazine*
WD: Wellington, 1st Duke of. *Dispatches of Field Marshal the Duke of Wellington*, ed. J. Gurwood, London 1834–8.

1. *USJ*, 1838, vol. III, p. 395.
2. In Beamish's edition of *Bismarck*, p. 134.
3. Cooper, T. H., p. 21.
4. *USJ*, 1831, vol. II, p. 182.
5. Dickinson, p. 5.
6. Leslie, p. 147.
7. Macdonald, J. E. J. A., vol. II, p. 55.
8. Clarendon, vol. III, p. 376.
9. Surtees, p. 22.
10. *WD*, vol. X, p. 458.
11. Hanger, *To All Sportsmen*, p. 205.
12. Verner, *Reminiscences*, p. 50.
13. Scharnhorst.
14. Henegan, vol. I, pp. 344–6.
15. Hanger, *Menaced Invasion*, p. 196.
16. From a tract published as an appendix to Robins.
17. *CUSM*, 1849, vol. I, p. 525.
18. *USM*, 1842, vol. I, p. 550.
19. Surtees, p. 22.
20. Anon, 'Seventy-First', p. 88.
21. Mercer, vol. I, p. 311.
22. Malcolm, p. 258.
23. Maxwell, vol. II, p. 137.
24. Hanger, *Menaced Invasion*, p. 151.
25. *USM*, 1843, vol. II, pp. 276–7.
26. *USJ*, 1834, vol. II, p. 323.
27. Surtees, p. 290.
28. *USM*, 1842, vol. I, p. 243.
29. Coignet, p. 76.
30. Fuller, Major-General J. F. C., 'Sir John Moore's Light Infantry Instructions of 1798–99', in *Journal of the Society for Army Historical Research*, 1952, vol. XXX, p. 75.
31. *USJ*, 1831, vol. II, p. 11.
32. *CUSM*, 1844, vol. III, p. 279.
33. *CUSM*, 1845, vol. I, p. 446.
34. Nicol, D., 'With Abercrombie and Moore in Egypt', in Low, p.63
35. Cadell, p. 96.
36. Simmons, p. 142.
37. *USJ*, 1838, vol. I, p. 246.
38. *London Chronicle*, 21 April 1796.
39. Lawrence, p. 216.
40. Anon., 'Forty-Third', p. 159.
41. 'General Hawley's "Chaos"', ed. Rev. P. Sumner, in *Journal of the Society for Army Historical Research*, 1948, vol. XXVI, p.93
42. Cotton, pp. 81–2.
43. *CUSM*, 1845, vol. I, p. 447.
44. *USM*, 1842, vol. I, p. 23.
45. *USJ*, 1834, vol. II, p. 320.
46. Anton, p. 196.
47. Austin, p. 90.
48. *WD*, vol. V, p. 85.
49. Las Cases, vol. IV, p. 143.
50. Bland, p. 157.
51. Kincaid, p. 276.
52. Aylmer Haly, in *BML*, vol. II, pp. 268–9.
53. *USJ*, 1841, vol. I, p. 472.
54. Geike, vol. I, p. 33.
55. Low, p. 30.
56. *CUSM*, 1846, vol. II, p. 240.
57. See Robson, *Road to Kabul*, pp. 224, 234.
58. Wheeler, p. 173.
59. Lawrence, pp. 147–8.
60. *USJ*, 1834, vol. II, p. 463.
61. Aitchison, p. 290.
62. *London Gazette*, 30 December 1813.
63. *USJ*, 1834, vol. II, p. 318.
64. MS account by an unidentified sergeant of the 1/2nd Foot Guards, author's possession.
65. Wood, p. 91.
66. Smith, p. 271.
67. Siborne, p. 341.
68. *USJ*, 1838, vol. I, p. 247.
69. *USJ*, 1840, vol. I, p. 535.
70. *USJ*, 1836, vol. III., p. 81.
71. Verner, *Rifle Brigade*, vol. II, p. 97.
72. Also spelled 'Plunkett'.
73. Beaufoy, p. 189.
74. Ibid., pp. 192–3.
75. *USJ*, 1831, vol. II, pp. 208–9.
76. *USM*, 1842, vol. III, p. 68.
77. *USJ*, 1831, vol. II, p. 11.
78. Sherer, p. 349.
79. Siborne, p. 408.
80. *USJ*, 1839, vol. III, pp. 249–50.
81. Ibid., p. 400.
82. This is one of several translations: *USJ*, 1834, vol. III, p. 397.
83. *USJ*, 1839, vol. III, p. 249.
84. Cooper, J. S., p. 82.
85. *USJ*, 1839, vol. III, p. 249.
86. *USJ*, 1836, vol. II, p. 200.
87. MacLeod, pp. 414–18.
88. *USJ*, 1838, vol. III, p. 241.
89. *USJ*, 1836, vol. III, p. 555.

90. *USJ*, 1839, vol. II. p. 400.

91. *USJ*, 1839, vol. I, p. 392.

92. *London Gazette*, 24 November 1810.

93. *USJ*, 1840, vol. I, p. 107.

94. Napier, Sir George, pp. 47–8.

95. Kincaid, p. 253.

96. *CUSM*, 1846, vol. II, p. 89.

97. Macdonald, R. J., p. 67.

98. *CUSM*, 1848, vol. III, pp. 29–30.

99. *Edinburgh Evening Courant*, 11 April 1814.

100. Ibid., 16 November 1812.

101. For a description of this scheme by a participant, see Frederiksen, J. C., 'The Letters of Captain John Scott', in *New Jersey History*, 1989, vol. 107, p. 71.

102. Alymer Haly, in *BML*, vol. II, p. 269.

103. *London Gazette*, 2 July 1811.

104. James, W., vol. II, p. 324.

105. Morley, p. 114.

106. Cooper, J. S., p. 28.

107. *USJ*, 1831, vol. II, p. 204.

108. *CUSM*, 1844, vol. III, p. 94.

109, *USJ*, 1834, vol. II pp. 555–6.

110. Mason.

111. Fuller, op. cit., p. 70.

112. Maude, p. 156.

113. Walter, p. 113.

114. *General Evening Post*, 22 January 1807.

115. Later Sir Kenneth Douglas of Glenbirvie, the name he adopted in 1830 upon elevation to a baronetcy.

116. Napier, Sir George, p. 13.

117. Ibid., p. 270.

118. Anon., *Volunteer Corps*, pp. 30–3.

119. Hanger, *Menaced Invasion*, pp. 159–60.

120. Cooper, T. H., pp. 16–17.

121. See Davidov, p. 76.

122. General Order, Brussels, 9 May 1815.

123. James, C., vol. II, p. 200.

124. *CUSM*, 1845, vol. I, p. 392.

125. *CUSM*, 1844, vol. III, p. 279.

126. Carter, pp. 82–3.

127. *BML*, vol. II, p. 367.

128 Dundas, p. 78.

129. Cooper, J. S., p. 85.

130. Coignet, pp. 117, 120.

131. Bland, p. 83.

132. Cooper, T. H., p. 22.

133. Dundas, p. 77.

134. *USJ*, 1834, vol. II, p. 471.

135. *CUSM*, 1845, vol. I, p. 403.

136. *Journal of the Royal Artillery*, 1907–8, vol. XXXIV, p. 554.

137. Oman, *Wellington's Army*, pp. 77–8.

138. Oman, *Studies*, pp. 33–72.

139. *WD*, vol. XII, p. 529.

140. *USM*, 1843, vol. II, p. 191.

141. Anon, 'Forty-Second', pp. 245–6.

142. Gleig, p. 100.

143. *The Courier*, 9 April 1811.

144. Surtees, p. 119.

145. *USJ*, 1841, vol. I, p. 539.

146. Lejeune, vol. I, p. 21.

147. *USJ*, 1838, vol. I, p. 108.

148. *BML*, vol. II, p. 269.

149. *USJ*, 1839, vol. I, p. 391.

150. Napier, Sir William, vol. I, pp. 258–9.

151. Siborne, p. 401.

152. Lieutenant George Pringle in ibid., p. 228.

153. Lieutenant Frederick Mainwaring in *CUSM*, 1844, vol. III, p. 410.

154. *USM*, 1843, vol. II, p. 192.

155. *USJ*, 1839, vol. III, p. 171.

156. Ibid., p. 248.

157. Austin, p. 126.

158. *USJ*, 1834, vol. II, p. 183.

159. *USJ*, 1834, vol. III, p. 397.

160. Ibid., pp. 505–7.

161. It appears in translation, for example, in Oman, *Wellington's Army*, pp. 91–2, and in Chandler, p. 348.

162. *CUSM*, 1844, vol. III, p. 92.

163. *CUSM*, 1845, vol. I, p. 403.

164. Sherer, p. 151.

165. Bland, p. 157.

166. Gleig, pp. 100–1.

167. Browne, p. 163, but note that the battalions concerned are misidentified: they were in fact the 3/27th and 1/40th.

168. *USJ*, 1839, vol. I, p. 392.

169. Napier, Sir William, vol. I, p. 258.

170. *USM*, 1843, vol. II, pp. 190–3.

171. Lejeune, vol. II, pp. 66–7.

172. *USJ*, 1839, vol. III, p. 170.

173. Ibid., p. 398.

174. Knowles, p. 27.

175. *USJ*, 1838, vol. I, p. 208.

176. *USJ*, 1831, vol. II, p. 181.

177. Afterwards Sir James Shaw Kennedy.

178. Shaw Kennedy, p. 101.

179. *USJ*, 1838, vol. III, p. 198.

180. Anton, pp. 193–4.

181. Tomkinson, p. 280.

182. *USJ*, 1840, vol. II, p. 477.

183. Cotton, p. 82.

184. Siborne, pp. 337–8.

185. *CUSM*, 1844, vol. I, p. 580.

186. Smith, pp. 278–9.

187. And now by the Royal Gloucestershire, Berkshire and Wiltshire Regiment.

188. Gleig, p. 184.

189. See Bodell, pp. 122–3.

BIBLIOGRAPHY

In addition to the works referred to in the Footnotes, this by no means exhaustive list includes some works of general relevance to the subject of Napoleonic weaponry and warfare.

Adye, R. W. *The Bombardier and Pocket Gunner*, 2nd rev. edn., London, 1802.

Aitchison, J. *An Ensign in the Peninsular War: The Letters of John Aitchison*, ed. W. K. F. Thompson, London, 1981.

Anon. *A Manual for Volunteer Corps of Infantry*, London, 1803.

Anon. *Memoirs of a Sergeant Late in the Forty-Third Light Infantry Regiment*, London, 1835.

Anon. *Personal Narrative of a Private Soldier who served in the Forty-Second Highlanders*, 1821.

Anon. *A Soldier of the Seventy-First*, ed. C. Hibbert, London 1975 (originally published 1819).

Anton, J. *Retrospect of a Military Life*, Edinburgh, 1841.

Ardant du Picq, C. J. J. J. *Battle Studies*, trans. J. N. Greely and R. C. Cotton, New York, 1921.

Austin, T. *Old Stick-Leg: Extracts from the Diaries of Major Thomas Austin*, ed. H. H. Austin, London, 1926.

Bailey, D. W. *British Military Longarms* 1715–1865, London, 1986.

Baker, E. *Remarks on Rifle Guns*, 11th edn., London, 1835.

Beaufoy, Captain H. *Scloppetaria, or Considerations on the Nature and Use of Rifled Barrel Guns*, London, 1808 (written under the nom-de-plume of 'A Corporal of Riflemen').

Bismarck, F. W. von. *Lectures on the Tactics of Cavalry*, trans. N. L. Beamish, London, 1827.

Blackmore, H. L. *British Military Firearms*, London, 1961.

Bland, H. *A Treatise of Military Discipline*, London, 1759 (originally published 1727).

Blaze, E. *Lights and Shades of Military Life*, ed. Sir Charles James Napier, London 1850, originally published as *La Vie Militaire sous le Premier Empire, ou Moeurs de garnison, du bivouac et de la caserne*, Paris 1837, reprinted *as Life in Napoleon's Army: the Memoirs of Elzéar Blaze*, London, 1995.

Bodell, J. *A Soldier's View of Empire: the Reminiscences of James Bodell* 1831–1892, ed. K. Sinclair, London, 1982.

Browne, T. H. *The Napoleonic War Journal of Captain Thomas Henry Browne* 1806–1816, ed. R. N. Buckley, London, 1987.

Cadell, Lieutenant-Colonel C. *Narrative of the Campaigns of the 28th Regiment since their return from Egypt in 1802*, London, 1835.

Carter, T. *Historical Record of the Forty-Fourth or East Essex Regiment*, Chatham, 1887.

Chandler, D. G. *The Campaigns of Napoleon*, London, 1967 (leading modern study).

Chartrand, R. *Uniforms and Equipment of the United States Forces in the War of 1812*, Youngstown, NY, 1992.

Clarendon, Earl of. *History of the Rebellion and Civil Wars in England*, ed. W. D. Macray, Oxford, 1888.

Coignet, J. R. *The Note-Books of Captain Coignet*, intro. Hon. Sir John Fortescue, London, 1929.

Colin, J. *La Tactique et la Discipline dans les Armées de la Révolution*, Paris 1902.

Cooper, J. S. *Rough Notes of Seven Campaigns in*

Portugal, Spain, France and America, Carlisle, 1869, r/p 1914.

Cooper, T. H. *A Practical Guide for the Light Infantry Officer*, London, 1806.

Cotton, E. *A Voice from Waterloo*, 9th edn., Brussels, 1900.

Darling, A. D. *Red Coat and Brown Bess*, Ottawa, 1970.

Davidov, D. *In the Service of the Tsar Against Napoleon*, trans. G. Troubetzkoy, London, 1999.

Dickinson, H. *Instructions for Forming a Regiment of Infantry ...*, London, 1798.

Duane, W. *The American Military Library*, Philadelphia, 1809.

Duffy, C. *Austerlitz*, London, 1977.

— *Borodino and the War of 1812*, London, 1972.

Dundas, Sir David. *Rules and Regulations for the Formation, Field-Exercise and Movements of His Majesty's Forces*, London, 1792, revd., 1798.

Elting, Colonel J. R. *Swords Around a Throne: Napoleon's Grande Armée*, London, 1989 (very important modern study).

Fletcher, I. *The Peninsular War: Aspects of the Struggle for the Iberian Peninsula*, Staplehurst, 1998; notably the essay by Paddy Griffith, 'Keep in step and they cannot hurt us: the Value of Drill in the Peninsular War'.

ffoulkes, C., and Hopkinson, E. C. *Sword, Lance and Bayonet*, Cambridge, 1938.

Geike, A. *Life of Sir Roderick Murchison Bart*, London, 1875.

Gleig, Revd G. R. *The Subaltern*, Edinburgh, 1872.

Glover, M. *Warfare in the Age of Bonaparte*, London, 1980.

Glover, R. *Peninsular Preparation: the Reform of the British Army 1795–1809*, Cambridge, 1963.

Griffith, P. *Forward into Battle: Fighting Tactics from Waterloo to Vietnam*, Chichester, 1981.

— *The Art of War in Revolutionary France 1789–1802*, London, 1998.

— (ed.) *A History of the Peninsular War vol. IX: Modern Studies of the War in Spain and Portugal 1808–1814*, London, 1999.

— (ed.) *Wellington Commander: The Iron Duke's Generalship*, Chichester, 1985.

Guy, A. J. (ed.) *The Road to Waterloo: The British Army and the Struggle Against Revolutionary and Napoleonic France, 1793–1815*, London, 1990.

Hanger, G. *Reflections on the Menaced Invasion*, London, 1804.

— *To All Sportsmen*, London, 1814.

Haythornthwaite, P. J. *The Armies of Wellington*, London, 1994.

— *The Napoleonic Source Book*, London, 1990.

— *Weapons and Equipment of the Napoleonic Wars*, Poole, 1979.

Henegan, R. *Seven Years' Campaigning in the Peninsula and the Netherlands from 1808 to 1815*, London, 1846.

Hicks, Major J. E. *French Military Weapons 1717–1938*, New Milford, Connecticut, 1964.

US Firearms 1776–1956, La Canada, California, 1957.

Hofschröer, P. *Prussian Light Infantry 1792–1815*, London, 1984.

Hughes, Major-General B. P. *Firepower: Weapons Effectiveness on the Battlefield 1630–1850*, London, 1974.

James, C. *The Regimental Companion*, London, 1804.

James, W. *The Naval History of Great Britain from the Declaration of War by France in 1793 to the Accession of George IV*, red. edn. London, 1878.

Jomini, H. A. *The Art of War*, London, 1862.

Kincaid, Sir John. *Adventures in the Rifle Brigade*, London 1830, and *Random Shots from a Rifleman*, London, 1835, r/p in comb. edn., London, 1908.

Knowles, R. *The War in the Peninsula: Some Letters of Lieutenant Robert Knowles*, ed. Sir Lees Knowles Bt., Bolton, 1913.

Las Cases, E. A. D. M. J. *Memoirs of the Life, Exile and Conversations of the Emperor Napoleon*, London, 1836.

Lavin, J. D. *History of Spanish Firearms*, London, 1965.

Lawrence, W. *The Autobiography of Sergeant William Lawrence*, ed. G. N. Bankes, London, 1886.

Lejeune, L. F. *Memoirs of Baron Lejeune*, trans. Mrs A. Bell, London, 1897.

Leslie, C. *Military Journal of Colonel Leslie, K.H., of Balquhain*, Aberdeen, 1887.

Low, E. B. *With Napoleon at Waterloo*, ed. McK. MacBride, London 1911.

Macdonald, J. E. J. A. *Recollections of Marshal Macdonald*, ed. C. Rousset, trans. S. L. Simeon, London, 1892.

Macdonald, R. J. *History of the Dress of the Royal Artillery*, London, 1899.

MacLeod, G. B. H. *Notes on the Surgery of the Crimean War*, London, 1858.

Malcolm, J. 'Reminiscences of a Campaign in the Pyrenees and South of France in 1814', in *Memorials of the Late War*, London 1831.

Marbot, J. B. A. M. *The Memoirs of Baron de Marbot*, trans. A. J. Butler, London, 1913.

Mason, R. O. *Pro Aris et Focis: Considerations ... for Reviving the use of the Long Bow with the Pike*, London, 1798.

Maude, F. N. *The Jena Campaign*, London, 1909.

Maxwell, Sir Herbert. *The Life of Wellington*, London, 1899.

Mercer, General A. C. *Journal of the Waterloo Campaign, Edinburgh and London*, 1870.

Mitchell, Colonel J. *Thoughts on Tactics and Military Organisation*, London, 1838.

Mollo, E. *Russian Military Swords*, London, 1969.

Morley, S. *Memoirs of a Serjeant of the 5th Regt. of Foot*, Ashford, 1842.

Müller, W. *Elements of the Science of War*, London, 1811.

Nafziger, G. F. *Imperial Bayonets: Tactics of the Napoleonic Battery, Battalion and Brigade as found in Contemporary Regulations*, London and Mechanicsburg, 1996 (important comparison and assessment of the various manoeuvre-regulations).

Napier, Sir George. *Passages in the Early Military Life of General Sir George T. Napier*, ed. General W. C. E. Napier, London, 1884.

Napier, Sir William. *History of the War in the Peninsula and South of France*, London, 1828–40.

Nosworthy, B. *Battle Tactics of Napoleon and his Enemies*, London, 1995 (important modern study).

Oman, Sir Charles. *History of the Peninsular War*, Oxford, 1902–30.

— *Wellington's Army*, London, 1912.

— *Studies in the Napoleonic Wars*, London, 1929.

Ottenfeld, R. von, and Teuber, O. *Die Oesterreichische Armee*, Vienna, 1895.

Priest, G. *The Brown Bess Bayonet 1720–1860*, Norwich, 1986.

Robins, B. *New Principles of Modern Gunnery*, London, 1805 (originally published 1742).

Robson, B. *Swords of the British Army*, London, 1975.

— *The Road to Kabul*, London, 1986.

Ross, S. T. *From Flintlock to Rifle: Infantry Tactics, 1740–1866*, London, 1996.

Rothenberg, G. E. *Napoleon's Great Adversaries: The Archduke Charles and the Austrian Army 1792–1814*, London, 1982.

The Art of War in the Age of Napoleon, London, 1977.

Scharnhorst, G. J. D. *Uber die Wirkung des*

Feuergewehrs, Berlin, 1813; a translation of these tests was published as *Results of Artillery and Infantry Gun Trials*, W. Leeson, Hemel Hempstead, 1992.

Shaw Kennedy, General Sir James. *Notes on the Battle of Waterloo*, London, 1865.

Sherer, M. *Recollections of the Peninsula*, London, 1823.

Siborne, Major-General H. T. (ed.) *The Waterloo Letters*, London, 1891.

Simmons, G. *A British Rifle Man*, ed. W. Verner, London, 1899.

Smith, Sir Harry. *The Autobiography of Sir Harry Smith*, ed. G. C. Moore Smith, London, 1902.

Strachan, H. *From Waterloo to Balaklava: Tactics, Technology and the British Army 1815–1854* (concerning the military developments which took place after the Napoleonic Wars, but also the lessons learned in those wars).

Surtees, W. *Twenty-Five Years in the Rifle Brigade*, London, 1833.

Tomkinson, W. *The Diary of a Cavalry Officer in the Peninsula and Waterloo Campaigns*, ed. J. Tomkinson, London, 1895.

Verner, W. *The Reminiscences of William Verner*, ed. R. W. Verner, London (SAHR) 1965.

Verner, Lieutenant-Colonel W. *History and Campaigns of the Rifle Brigade, 1809–1813*, London, 1919.

Wagner, E. *Cut and Thrust Weapons*, Prague and London, 1967.

Walter, J. *The Volunteer Force*, London, 1881.

Wheeler, W. *The Letters of Private Wheeler, 1809–1828*, ed. B. H. Liddell Hart, London, 1951.

Wood, C. *The Subaltern Officer*, London, 1825.

PERIODICALS

Many periodicals contain material relevant to the subject of Napoleonic tactics and weaponry, including a number devoted exclusively to the Napoleonic period. Many of the more general periodicals also contain articles of relevance, including the journals of learned societies such as the *Carnet de la Sabretache* or the *Journal of the Society for Army Historical Research* (in addition to material listed in the footnotes, for example, the latter includes a paper of particular relevance to the subject of this book: J. R. Arnold, 'A Reappraisal of Column versus Line in the Napoleonic Wars', in vol. LX, 1982, pp. 196–208). Other material can be found in commercial publications such as the *British Military Illustrated* or the French *Uniformes* (ex-*Gazette des Uniformes*) and *Tradition*. Among those concerned with 'minor tactics' was the journal of the New Jersey Association of Wargamers, *Empires, Eagles and Lions*, originally published in Cambridge, Ontario, which presented much contemporary information and discussion.

INDEX